Caroline Hadley

Half Hours with the Bible

Caroline Hadley

Half Hours with the Bible

ISBN/EAN: 9783337851156

Printed in Europe, USA, Canada, Australia, Japan

Cover: Foto ©Lupo / pixelio.de

More available books at **www.hansebooks.com**

HALF HOURS WITH THE BIBLE;

OR,

The Children's Scripture Story-Book.

AN EPITOME OF THE HISTORIES

CONTAINED IN

THE OLD AND NEW TESTAMENT,

SIMPLIFIED FOR THE USE OF CHILDREN.

BY THE AUTHOR OF "HAPPY SUNDAYS."

With above 150 Illustrative Engravings.

NEW YORK:
McLOUGHLIN BROTHERS.

CONTENTS.

		PAGE
1.	THE CREATION OF THE WORLD AND THE DELUGE	9
2.	STORIES OF ABRAHAM, ISAAC, AND JACOB	41
3.	JOSEPH AND HIS BRETHREN	73
4.	THE HISTORY OF MOSES AND OF THE WANDERINGS OF THE CHILDREN OF ISRAEL IN THE DESERT	105
5.	THE JUDGES AND MIGHTY MEN OF OLD	137
6.	THE KINGS OF ISRAEL AND JUDAH	169
7.	THE PROPHETS	201
8.	THE GOOD CHILDREN OF SCRIPTURE	233
9.	THE LIFE OF JESUS CHRIST, OUR SAVIOUR	265
10.	OUR SAVIOUR'S TEACHINGS AND SUFFERINGS	297
11.	THE STORY OF THE APOSTLES	329

PREFACE.

THE object of the Author of this little book has been to tell, in plain, simple words that may be readily understood by children, the mighty histories contained in the Sacred Volume.

It will be seen that the work has been carefully divided into sections of equal length, each embracing a separate portion of the Bible, and complete in itself. Thus, the first part contains the History of the Creation, the Fall of Man, and the subsequent events until the time of the Deluge; the second part is devoted to the History of the Patriarchs, Abraham, Isaac, and Jacob; the third, to the History of Joseph and his brethren; the fourth, to the History of Moses and the Wanderings of the Children of Israel, until the time of their great leader's death. And thus the history proceeds through the times of the Judges, the Kings, and the Prophets; just so much being given as a child may understand and remember, and the whole being divided, like the commencement of the book, into short sections, to prevent confusion. The three last parts are devoted to the narration of the Life of Our Saviour and of the Apostles.

As the book purposes to give to children an elementary knowledge of the narrative portion of the Scriptures, care has been taken to tell the stories as much as possible in the "Bible words." A few sentences of explanation or of comment have been sparingly introduced—the Author

viii   PREFACE.

having, in the great majority of cases, thought it best simply to narrate the histories as intelligibly as possible, leaving them to make their own unfailing impression on the minds of the young readers.

Thus, then, this little volume is addressed to no special sect or denomination. It has not been prepared with any particular reference to the evangelical, the high church, or the dissenting part of the community. Free from all sectarian doctrine, and holding aloof from the exclusive tenets of any particular sect, it aims at being emphatically a Child's History of the Bible. Therefore it is broadly offered to all that great and happily increasing class who read and value the Sacred Book, and wish their children to read and value it also. Therefore, the histories have been presented in all their touching simplicity—therefore the *Bible words* have, so far as possible, been retained.

It has been the wish of the Publishers to increase the attractions of the volume by care in the production of the work, so far as paper and print are concerned, and by a plentiful supply of those "pictures" in which all children delight.

The Author commends this Book, the result of many hours of pleasant labor, to the parents, and yet more to the children of Christendom; and a careful perusal, undertaken at the request of the Publishers, has convinced me that the task has been well and conscientiously fulfilled.

                                                                    H. W. D.

Half Hours with the Bible.

THE CREATION OF THE WORLD AND THE DELUGE.

CHAPTER I.

THE CREATION OF THE WORLD.

THE Bible is that large book from which the minister reads in church every Sunday. It tells us of the doings of the great God who made Heaven and Earth; and from it we learn to love and to serve Him. The word Bible means "The Book." The Bible was written at different times by wise and good men, who set down the words that God put into their minds; so that the Bible is the written word of God Himself. That is why the Bible is called *the* Book of Books; and its words are the words of truth. There was not always a Bible, to teach us about

God; but there was always a God. He had no beginning, but always was, and is, and shall be, after this world has passed away. He it was who made us, who created this beautiful world, and all that it contains. It was God who put it into the minds of good men to write down in this holy Book, called the Bible, all the wondrous things of His law. And, as the Bible tells us of God, and teaches us His will, therefore every one should strive to learn to read this good Book; and there is such a wonderful amount of wisdom and goodness in it, that the smallest child may read parts of it with delight and wonder. God loves little children, and never forgets or forsakes them. There are, however, many things in this Sacred Volume which you could not understand; and, therefore, it is very pleasant to be told, in easy words, what wonderful things God has done. This, my dear children, is what I wish to do for you in this little book of Bible Stories and Pictures; and I am sure it will make you long for the time when you may read the Great Book for yourselves.

The Bible tells us that in the beginning God created the heaven and the earth. He *created* them; that means, he made them out of nothing. There was no shape, nor form, only thick darkness, until "the Spirit of God moved upon the face of the waters." God said, Let there be light; and there was light.

Is it not wonderful that the word of God should at once change darkness into light? And how beautiful is

THE CREATION OF THE WORLD AND THE DELUGE. 11

THE SEPARATION OF THE WATERS.

light! Darkness is very mournful. Many little children are afraid of being left in the dark, although there is nothing that would hurt them in the dark any more than in the light, because God can see in the dark as well as by day, and can take care of us. Yet light is a great blessing, and we ought to thank God for it.

"And God saw the light that it was good: and God

divided the light from the darkness." The light He called Day, and the darkness He called Night. "And the evening and the morning were the first day." In six days God made the earth; and on the second day He made the firmament, and divided the waters which were under the firmament from the waters which were above the firmament. On the third day God separated the land from the waters, and gathered the waters together upon an heap, calling them Seas; while the dry land He called Earth. And at His word the earth brought forth grass, herbs, and trees of all kinds. On the fourth day God created the greater light, that is, the sun, to rule the day, and the lesser light, or moon, to rule the night; and He made the stars also.

> "First, He made the sun to know
> His proper hour to rise;
> And to give light to all below,
> Did send him round the skies."

And since that day, obedient to God's command, the sun has risen every morning, and set every evening; and so long as God commands, and no longer, will the sun continue to blaze in the sky.

The moon, too, with her soft, silvery light, God created, to shine while we are asleep; and the pretty twinkling stars did God set in the firmament, to shed light upon the earth. Then God commanded the waters to bring forth abundantly every kind of fish, and fowl that may fly above the earth. Fishes of all kinds, from the great whale, that taketh his pastime in the wide ocean, to the little minnow

that sports in the shallowest stream;—from the ostrich to the little wren that builds her nest in an old thornbush. God also bade the earth to bring forth cattle, creeping things, and beasts of all kinds; and there, side by side, might be seen the great elephant, the useful ox, the timid hare, and the gliding, harmless worm. This was the work of the fifth day, and God saw that it was good.

So now, God had created the world; but the greatest and most wonderful of created beings had not yet been made. The earth was there, and the ocean; both full of living

creatures, and gay with growing plants and grasses. The streams were flowing, and the birds singing, and the fishes glancing through the waters, and the great beasts stalking forth over the face of the green earth, and all the little insects sporting in the sunshine; all was ready for the reception of him whom God had determined to make the king of this beautiful creation—and this wondrous being was man.

And the sixth day of creation had come: and God said, "Let us make man in our own image, after our likeness, and let them have dominion over the fish of the sea, and over the fowl of the air, and over the cattle, and over all the earth, and over every creeping thing that creepeth upon the earth." So God created man out of the dust of the earth, in His own image created He him. And God breathed into his nostrils the breath of life; and man became a living soul. And God bade him be fruitful and multiply, and fill the earth, and subdue it; and He gave him dominion over every living thing that moveth upon the earth. And God said, "Behold, I have given you every herb," and "every tree yielding fruit, to you it shall be for meat." And to the beast, to the fowls, and all other living creatures God gave every green herb for meat.

And thus, day after day, God still provides us with all things necessary for our support: and He it is who, by His Son Jesus Christ, has Himself taught us to say, "Give us this day our daily bread." He it is who makes the corn to grow, and to ripen, that we may be supplied with daily food.

When God had created the heavens, and the earth, and all the host of them, He finished His work and rested upon the seventh day; and He blessed the seventh day, and sanctified it, or made it holy, because in it He rested from all His work that He had created, or made. Wherefore, God afterwards gave a command to His favored people, the Jews, saying, "Remember that thou keep holy the Sabbath day." And, therefore, to the present time, in all lands where God is known, and the Bible, His word, is read, one day out of every seven is set apart and kept holy, as a remembrance that God rested on the seventh day from His work, after the creation of the world.

And God looked down from heaven on everything that He had made; and behold, it was very good.

THE CREATION OF THE WORLD AND THE DELUGE.

ADAM NAMING THE BEASTS.

CHAPTER II.
THE FALL OF ADAM AND EVE.

THE Bible next tells us about the Garden of Eden, and how the man whom God had created was sent to live there. First of all, now that the herbs and trees were growing, God caused a mist to go up from the earth, and watered the whole face of the ground.

And God then planted a fair and a fruitful garden in Eden, and watered it with beautiful rivers and cooling streams, and placed man in the garden to keep it and to dress it. This man was called Adam. He was formed after God's image, perfectly holy and perfectly happy, free from care and free from sin.

Although God had made him lord over all things that He had created, yet, among all these things, none was found that was fit to be a companion for Adam. So the Lord God said: "It is not good that the man should be alone; I will make him an help meet for him." And God brought every living thing to Adam, to see what name Adam would call them; and whatsoever Adam called every living creature was henceforth the name thereof. God caused Adam to fall into a deep sleep; and, while he slept, God took from Adam's side one of his ribs, and of the man's rib God formed a woman, and brought her unto the man. And Adam called her *woman;* and she became the wife of Adam, and the mother of all living, which her name, *Eve*, signifies.

When the Lord God placed man in the lovely and pleasant garden of Eden, He gave Adam leave to eat of the fruit of every tree except one, which God told him was the tree of the knowledge of good and evil, and of this tree God forbade Adam to eat; and God told him plainly, that if he ate of the fruit of this tree, he should surely die; and as Adam had everything that was needful for his use, there was no reason why he should want this fruit.

Adam and Eve might have continued holy and happy for ever, for their life was bright, and innocent, and blessed in the beautiful garden, with the smile of God upon them; but there came a wicked spirit, called Satan, who is the father of lies, and of all evil. He was envious when he saw the man and his wife so happy; so he came in the form of a serpent, and talked with Eve, and persuaded her to eat of the forbidden fruit. The woman told the serpent that God had threatened them with death if they ate of the fruit of that tree; but the wily serpent answered, "Ye shall not surely die: for God doth know that in the day ye eat thereof, then your eyes shall be opened, and ye shall be as gods, knowing good and evil." See how wily the serpent was; he knew that the prospect of great knowledge, and of being as a god, would allure Eve.

And it was so. She listened to the tempter. Instead of being contented in the happy state in which God had placed her, she became covetous. She wanted to be wiser and greater than she was. She took the fruit of the tree which God had forbidden her to eat, and she gave her husband some of the fruit, and he ate also.

When they had done this, they felt afraid. The knowledge that came to them was the knowledge that they themselves were no longer good and innocent; and they feared to meet the eye of God. They sewed large fig leaves together to make themselves a covering. And when they heard the voice of the Lord in the garden, in the cool of the day, fearful to meet Him, as they well might be they vainly endeavored to hide themselves among the trees

ADAM AND EVE EATING THE FORBIDDEN FRUIT.

And God called to Adam: "Where art thou?" And Adam answered, that he had hidden himself, because he was afraid. God knew perfectly well what they had done; but He asked Adam if he had eaten of the forbidden fruit? And Adam was cowardly, and answered, that *the woman* had given him the fruit; for he would gladly have laid the whole blame upon Eve.

THE CREATION OF THE WORLD AND THE DELUGE. 21

And when God asked Eve, why she had done this, she answered, that the serpent had beguiled her. Then God pronounced the sentence of punishment upon them all. He cursed the serpent above every beast of the field, and told him he should always crawl upon the earth. The woman

ADAM AND EVE DRIVEN FROM THE GARDEN OF EDEN.

he condemned to a life of sorrow and pain. And to Adam God said, "In the sweat of thy face shalt thou eat bread, till thou return unto the ground; for out of it wast thou taken, and unto dust thou shalt return."

So God sent forth Adam and Eve from the garden of Eden; and God placed at the east end of the garden cherubims, or angels of fire, with a flaming sword, which turned every way, to keep the way of the tree of life. So they were never again permitted to enter the lovely garden, but they were obliged to work hard and till the ground, and to plant and sow, and dig up the thistles, until the time should come for them to die, and return to the dust.

CHAPTER III.

CAIN AND ABEL.

AFTER our first parents had been driven out of the pleasant garden of Eden, God gave a little son to Eve, who called his name Cain. Afterwards she had a second son, named Abel. God had said to Adam that man should eat bread in the sweat of his brow—that is, that he should earn his food by labor. So both these sons were brought up to work;—and this was right; for it is God's will that every one should work in some way, and it is a great sin to be idle. Even the rich people, who need not till the ground for their bread, should find something useful to do for God, or for their neighbors.

THE CREATION OF THE WORLD AND THE DELUGE. 23

ADAM AND EVE AT WORK.

Not even a little child should be idle. Children should be learning, while they are young, how to employ their time, so that they may spend it usefully when they grow older. Cain used to till the ground and sow the seed, that there might be plenty of food. He was what we call a husbandman. Abel took care of a flock of sheep. He was what we now call a shepherd. I dare say you know who said, "I am the good Shepherd, and know my sheep, and am known of mine." Our Lord Jesus Christ is the good Shepherd, and those children who strive to please Him, and learn to love Him as sheep love their shepherd, are those He means when He talks of His lambs.

CAIN KILLING ABEL.

Now, God had commanded his servants to offer up a sacrifice to Him of the "first-fruits;" that is, something of the very best they had. But He not only required these offerings, but He wished them to be given to Him with a free heart, and a willing, humble spirit. Cain brought an offering to the Lord, of the first-fruits of the ground, and

THE CREATION OF THE WORLD AND THE DELUGE.

Abel brought of the firstlings of his flock; and the Lord had respect unto Abel and his offering; that is to say, He looked upon them with favor, for He knew Abel offered with a thankful spirit. But unto Cain and to his offering He had not respect. See how the smoke of Abel's lamb ascends steadily up to heaven, while that of Cain is beaten down to the earth.

God read the wicked thoughts that were in Cain's heart, and saw that he was envious and jealous of his good and gentle brother: and when Cain found that the Lord had accepted the offering of his brother, and not his own, he became still more angry. And when they were both together in the field, he rose up against his brother and slew him!

* * * *

Adam and Eve were sorry for their own sin and disobedience, when they saw that *Death*, the punishment with which they had been threatened, had really come upon their young and cherished son. He was dead, and he had been killed by the act of Cain: and the punishment of their own sin and disobedience was falling heavily upon them. But God, who sees and knows all things, saw this wicked deed; and He called unto Cain, and said, "Where is Abel thy brother?" Cain knew not how to answer; the cowardly, guilty man replied by a lie. He said, "I know not: am I my brother's keeper?" Then the Lord said,

"What hast thou done? the voice of thy brother's blood crieth unto me from the ground." And God told Cain that a fearful punishment should befall him for his dreadful crime. He said, "When thou tillest the ground, it shall no more yield unto thee strength," or increase. And Cain was to be a wanderer and an outcast on the earth. And when Cain heard the words of the Lord, and found that he must leave his parents, and be driven out as a vagabond, he said, "My punishment is greater than I can bear." So God drove him away from his parents, and he dwelt in a distant part of the earth; where we hear that he built a city, and that sons and daughters were born unto him. But the remembrance of Cain's crime has never passed away, for it has been written by God's servants, in God's own Book; and, as long as this world lasts, Cain will be spoken of as the unhappy man who killed his brother in his anger.

CHAPTER IV.

THE FLOOD.

AFTER the death of Abel, God comforted Adam and Eve by giving them a son, named Seth. And, in time, Seth grew to be a man, and had sons and daughters of his own. One of his descendants was named Enoch. Of Enoch, we have an account in the Bible. We are told that he was a good man, and walked with God—that is, he obeyed His commands. So God took him up into heaven without dying. What a difference between his fate and that of Cain!

Enoch's son, Methuselah, was the oldest man that ever lived on the earth. He was nearly a thousand years old when he died. After this time, the people who lived in those days became very wicked, and their conduct displeased the Lord so much, that He repented that He had made man. And at length He determined to destroy them all by a great flood. There was, however, a good man called Noah, who found grace in the eyes of the Lord. And God commanded Noah to build him an ark of gopher wood; and told him how long and how broad it was to be, and how to build it, that Noah and his family might be safe, when God should send the flood of waters to drown the world.

A very wonderful building was the ark which God commanded Noah to build for the safety of himself and family, and all the living creatures that God intended to save alive: two of every kind, as you see them going into the ark. Noah had nothing to do but to obey God's directions, and he did so. He began at once to collect proper materials; and for a hundred years he was preaching to his neighbors and friends, begging them to turn from their sin, and help him to prepare the ark that was to save the righteous from destruction. But no one would listen; they only laughed at Noah for his folly, when he told them that God had said, "I will bring a flood of waters upon the earth, to destroy all flesh, wherein is the breath of life, from under heaven; and every thing that is in the earth shall die. But with thee will I establish my covenant; and thou shalt come into the ark, thou, and thy sons, and thy wife, and thy sons' wives with thee. And of every living thing of all flesh, two of every sort shalt thou bring into the ark, to keep them alive with thee; they shall be male and female." Of fowls also, and cattle, and every creeping thing, two of every sort, did God order Noah to take with him into the ark, and to take some of every kind of food that was necessary for them all to eat, to gather together a large portion to place in the ark. How mercifully God still showed his love and care of those creatures whom He intended to spare; providing for all their necessities, and giving them light, and air, and pleasant food!

THE CREATION OF THE WORLD AND THE DELUGE.   29

NOAH PRAYING, BEFORE ENTERING THE ARK.

Such was the refuge God provided for His servant Noah and his family; and He has shown similar mercy to the whole of mankind. For God has provided another ark, or place of safety, for lost and ruined sinners; and when God looks down now from His holy dwelling-place in heaven, He can see that even the very thoughts of men's hearts are desperately wicked; and, therefore, He has provided an ark for these perishing souls to flee to. Do you know what that ark is called? It is the Holy Saviour

Jesus Christ; the only offer'ng which the world could produce to appease the just anger of an offended God. He provided the ark; and the same love provided the Saviour, the ark of our strength—the refuge from the storm of trouble and the flood of sin. He has in Himself all things necessary for our support and salvation, just as the ark contained all that was necessary for Noah and his family.

Many years was the ark building. Long it stood open, while Noah vainly tried to persuade the hardened sinners to enter the door. So Christ is always ready, always at hand to save; he stands waiting, he is willing and able to save all who will go unto him. Like a tender father, God said to Noah, when all was ready, "Come thou and all thy house into the ark; for thee have I seen righteous before me." So Noah obeyed, as a child should obey the voice of his parent; and he made all the animals that he had collected together to enter two and two into the ark, and then he went in, with all the members of his family; and God shut them in.

And then God in his anger rained down rain from heaven, and the waters of the sea overflowed and spread over the earth, till by degrees the houses, the trees, and even the tops of the highest mountains, were covered with deep water. The rain lasted for forty days and forty nights, and the whole world was like a tempestuous sea, which washed away every living thing. Even the birds of the air were drowned, for there was nothing left on

THE CREATION OF THE WORLD AND THE DELUGE. 31

THE GREAT FLOOD OF WATERS.

which they might rest the soles of their feet; and when the rain ceased to fall, it was many days and weeks before the waters dried away from the face of the earth. Only Noah and his family were safe in the ark which God had provided for them.

At length the rain ceased, the waters abated, and the ark rested on the top of a mountain called Ararat; and Noah opened the window. There was still nothing but a waste of waters: no green trees or flowers, no living creature to be seen. But Noah sent out of the ark a raven and a dove. The raven flew backwards and forwards, and at last disappeared. Perhaps some of the dead bodies of the animals had floated up to the top of the mountain, and they would provide food for the raven, which is a bird of prey; but the poor dove could find no rest for the sole of her foot, so she returned to the ark, and Noah put out his hand and took her in to him again.

Seven days after, Noah sent the dove out again; in the evening she returned to him with an olive leaf in her beak. You may be sure Noah and his sons were glad to see this green leaf. They knew that the tops of the trees were again visible, and that the waters were abating. But they knew the earth was still under water, because the dove was unable to find food and shelter; and therefore they waited patiently, and thanked God for his mercy in giving them a roof to cover them, and food to sustain life.

The dove was sent out once again; but she returned no more. Then Noah knew that the earth was getting dry. He took the covering off the ark, and felt very glad to look upon the green trees; but, although they had been shut up in the ark for more than a year, and although the earth looked dry and pleasant, Noah did not wish to go out of the ark until God told him he might do so. But "God spake unto Noah, saying, Go forth of the ark, thou, and thy wife, and thy sons, and thy sons' wives with thee. Bring forth with thee every living thing that is with thee,

THE CREATION OF THE WORLD AND THE DELUGE.

of all flesh, both of fowl, and of cattle, and of every creeping thing that creepeth upon the earth; that they may breed abundantly in the earth, and be fruitful, and multiply upon the earth."

"And Noah went forth, and his sons, and his wife, and his sons' wives with him;—every beast, every creeping thing, and every fowl, and whatsoever creepeth upon the earth, after their kinds, went forth out of the ark."

And so God's justice and God's mercy had both been shown: His justice in the great deluge, and His mercy in the preservation of Noah and his family.

DOVE AND RAVEN.

CHAPTER V.

NOAH'S SACRIFICE, AND THE RAINBOW.

THE first thing Noah did when they were all come out of the ark was to build an altar unto the Lord; and he took one of every clean beast and every clean fowl, and offered them as burnt offerings upon the altar. Was it not right to Noah to show his gratitude to the good God who had preserved him and his family from a dreadful death? And ought we not also to love Him who preserves us and gives us so many blessings? Noah thought of heaven and of God's mercy to him and his family, while he offered his burnt sacrifices, and the perfume of these offerings went up to heaven. "And the Lord said in his heart, I will not again curse the ground any more for man's sake; for the imagination of man's heart is evil from his youth; neither will I again smite any more every thing living as I have done. While the earth remaineth, seed time and harvest, and cold and heat, and summer and winter, and day and night shall not cease."

And God's promises never fail: although thousands of years have passed away, still the seasons follow in succession. The sun shines by day, and the bright stars twinkle in the dark blue sky at night, as they did when God made his covenant with Noah.

THE CREATION OF THE WORLD AND THE DELUGE.   35

NOAH'S SACRIFICE.

"And God said, This is the token of the covenant which I make between me and you and every living creature that is with you, for perpetual generations; I do set my *bow* in the cloud, and it shall be for a token of a covenant between me and the earth. And it shall come to pass, when I bring a cloud over the earth, that the bow shall be seen in the cloud: and I will remember my covenant, which is between me and you and every living creature of all flesh; and the waters shall no more become a flood to destroy all flesh. And the bow shall be in the cloud; and I will look upon it, that I may remember the everlasting covenant between God and every living creature of all flesh that is upon the earth."

How often have my little readers beheld this token of God's mercy and forbearance—the beautiful rainbow, spanning the sky like an arch, and brightening the dark clouds with its soft and lovely tints of various colors! Whenever you see this pretty bow, look at it well, and think that God has placed that rainbow in the heavens to remind you and all the world that He is faithful and gracious; and that Jesus, who is far more lovely than the rainbow, sits upon a throne encircled with a rainbow; and that, although we cannot see him, he is there; and let the storm be ever so violent, his protecting hand is stretched out to save those that love and trust in him.

When Noah and his sons had sacrificed to God, they went away into different places, and made themselves homes, and God gave them many children, so that the earth was soon full of people again; and they cultivated their lands, and planted vineyards and fruit trees. And God blessed Shem and Japheth, because they were dutiful to their father; and he blessed Noah, and lengthened his life three hundred and fifty years after the flood. The Bible gives us the names of the grandsons and great grandsons of this good man.

CHAPTER VI.

THE TOWER OF BABEL.

FOR many years after the deluge all the people in the world spoke but one language; but as they, by degrees, forgot God's mercy to their forefathers in saving them from the flood, they became proud and self-willed, and at last they determined to build a tower that would reach unto heaven. Nimrod, their leader, had built a large city, called Babel; and then they wanted a tower.

But these people well knew they were wrong; their consciences told them that their conduct was displeasing to God, and that they knew they deserved to be punished; and their own words prove that they felt afraid of God's just anger, for they said—" A tower, whose top may reach unto heaven; lest we be scattered abroad upon the face of the earth." Now, if they had loved and trusted in God, they would have been happy and contented; but, instead of that, they were in fear of some unseen, but not undeserved calamity, and tried to set themselves up against God. They thought if they could build a tower whose top should reach to heaven, they could escape, if another flood came upon the earth, by climbing up to the top. They cared not about going to heaven by the narrow path of faith,

38 HALF HOURS WITH THE BIBLE.

BUILDING OF THE TOWER OF BABEL.

and honesty, and self-denial; no, they must make themselves bricks, and burn them thoroughly. They found out a means of mixing clay and straw, and moulding them into bricks, which they burned till they were hard, and they used a kind of slime for mortar; and, in order to make themselves a great name, they worked hard, piling up their bricks and mortar story above story, hoping to get out of the reach of God's judgments; forgetting that God was

THE CREATION OF THE WORLD AND THE DELUGE.

above all, and could see all they did and planned, and even their very thoughts. The Lord let them go on for some time in their boastfulness and pride.

Then the Lord came down to see the city and the tower, which the children of men builded. And the Lord said, "Behold the people is one, and they have all one language; and this they begin to do: and now nothing will be restrained from them, which they have imagined to do." And God said, "Let us confound their language, that they may not understand one another's speech." All at once they began to call things by different names. They could no longer call each other by their names. One was speaking in one tongue, another in a different language. None could understand, nor could others reply; so they were obliged to leave off building; the work on which they prided themselves so much was left unfinished; their names are forgotten; and the story of their great undertaking is only told to their shame.

Truly God He is the judge, and He only suffers what He will to be executed; and, to show us this truth, He has ordained that the errors, the sin, and the punishment of our forefathers should be written in the Holy Bible, as a guide and warning to all who shall come after. And, while we pride ourselves upon our learning, upon our being able to speak and understand the language of other countries, let us remember that sin occasioned the first differences in our tongue and speech; that God in his anger said, "Let us confound their language, that they may not understand one another's speech : and the Lord scattered them abroad upon the face of all the earth;" wherefore the name of that city and tower is called Babel (which means confusion); "because the Lord did there confound the language of the earth: and from thence did the Lord scatter them abroad upon the face of the earth."

More than once God changed the language of people in one moment. The first time He did it as a proof of His displeasure, and to prevent the people from understanding each other's words and wishes. The second time it was a proof of God's mercy. He gave to the Apostles, who were ignorant, uneducated men, all in one minute, the power of preaching in other tongues the Gospel of Christ. Miraculous tongues came like tongues of fire, and sat upon the heads of his humble disciples, and they were able to go forth into other lands, and tell the blessed truths of salvation to those who were in darkness and in sin. May we all attend to these warnings, and acknowledge God's power to punish pride, and to reward and bless the humble and meek.

Half Hours with the Bible.

STORIES OF ABRAHAM, ISAAC, AND JACOB

CHAPTER I.

ABRAHAM, SARAH, AND ISHMAEL.

VERY wonderful is the flight of time; day follows night, and night follows day, and one season succeeds another; and the sun appears to move on, and the earth turns round, and every day brings change.

You, who are now children, will in time be old people, and you will die, to make room for others who will live in your places. And if you ever think of these marvels, you may perhaps sometimes think about those who lived a great many years before you were born. In the Bible we can read the history of persons who, like us, descended from Adam and Eve; some who were tempted and fell into sin, or others who resisted the temptations of Satan to forsake what was right, and who loved and obeyed God. We there perceive that all who sinned deliberately or intentionally were punished according to the threats uttered by the ever-present God; and those who were obedient to his laws received the promises.

Abram was a man who, for his belief in God's words, and his ready and willing services, was called the "father of the faithful." He was born about three hundred years after the flood; and when about seventy years old he was commanded by God to leave the land of his birth and go to another country, which the Lord then promised to give to his children for an inheritance; and there he foretold that his children should be afflicted and carried into a strange country, where they should suffer many hardships; but that after four hundred years he would give them the whole country of Canaan.

Abram, finding that God gave no children to his wife Sarai, followed the custom of the country, and took Sarai's maid to be his wife; and God gave her a son, named Ishmael. Before the birth of her child, however, Hagar forgot her duties to her mistress. This made Sarai treat Hagar unkindly, until Hagar, in anger and sorrow, determined to run away; so she fled into the wilderness. Poor Hagar went away into a wild country, were there were no houses nor people for many miles; and she was a stranger in the land, having nowhere to go, so she strayed about in

SARAI'S UNKINDLY TREATMENT TOWARDS HAGAR.

the wilderness until she found a well of water; and there, tired and weary, she sat down. Perhaps she began to think she had done wrong, and been proud and wilful, and to feel sorry for it; and, perhaps, she prayed to God to forgive her and take care of her; for we read that an angel of the Lord was sent to comfort her. He told her that she should be the mother of a son, who would be the father of a great nation; but that he would be a wild man, that his hand should be against every man, and every man's hand against him; meaning that he would live a wandering life, and exist upon spoil, and on what he could get by hunting and warfare. From Ishmael, whose name signifies "God will hear," are descended the people of Arabia, and they live in the deserts of Arabia, in tents, and travel on camels and horses from place to place, in search of food and plunder.

The angel also commanded Hagar to return to her mistress, and submit to her in all things, as was becoming in a servant. So Hagar was comforted and went back to Sarai, who, most likely, received her with kindness. We must never forget, when we are unhappy, or think ourselves unkindly used by others, to pray to God for help. He can see and know all that can happen to us; and He can comfort us when He has seen how we bear the trials He thinks proper to send upon us. It is of no use to try to run away from Him Hagar acknowledged this when the angel spoke to her; she knew directly that God had found her out, and she said at once, "Thou God seest me." Oh, if we could always remember that God can see, and know, and remember everything we do and say, we should be more careful not to do wrong, and we should at all times be anxious to do what was right in his eyes.

Soon after the birth of Ishmael, God changed the names of Abram and Sarai. The Lord called her Sarah, which signifies "a princess," and Abram was to be called Abraham, which means "the father of a multitude." And God made a covenant or agreement with Abraham, as he had with Noah about the flood; and with Adam, when he promised that he would send a Saviour, who should be of the seed of the woman. And this Saviour was to descend from Abraham and Sarah, as we shall read hereafter

CHAPTER II.

SODOM AND GOMORRAH.

LOT, the son of Haran, Abraham's brother, had gone to live at a city called Sodom, and near Gomorrah, another large and populous city. The people in these cities had become so bad that God determined to send down fire from heaven and destroy them all. But he would not do this until he had told Abraham what he intended to do. So one day, when Abraham was sitting at the door of his tent, three men appeared to him, one of whom was the Lord Jesus. Yes, Jesus lived in heaven before he came upon earth. Abraham did not know them; but he spoke respectfully to them, and begged them to come in, and he provided for them a meal of the best things that he had, and Sarah baked cakes for them, and they did eat; after which they promised that Sarah, who was now an old woman, should have a son.

At first Sarah laughed at these words, because she thought they were only joking, but she afterwards believed. The two angels then went towards Sodom, and the Lord stayed with Abraham, and told him that he was going to destroy these cities. Abraham remembered Lot, and hoped that he had not become wicked, but rather that he had taught all his family and servants to serve God. His kind heart was touched with fear, lest Lot might be destroyed with the wicked people among whom he dwelt; so he prayed to God to spare the city if fifty righteous people should be found therein. And God promised to spare the city if there should be fifty righteous people in it. Then Abraham begged him for the sake of forty; then for thirty; then for twenty. And the Lord hearkened, and promised that he would spare the cities if there could be found only ten good men therein. But not even the ten were found. Although the Lord had determined to destroy the cities, he remembered the prayer of Abraham, and he spared the life of Lot. The two angels came into Sodom, and they found Lot sitting at the gate of the city; and he arose and bowed himself before them, and invited them to go and sleep at his house; for it was now evening, and he thought they were travellers and strangers in that country. You see

STORIES OF ABRAHAM, ISAAC, AND JACOB.   47

THE DESTRUCTION OF SODOM AND FATE OF LOT'S WIFE.

Lot was kind and hospitable; and he set supper before them. They then desired Lot to gather together all the members of his family, and to hasten and take them all with him out of the city, for the Lord was going to destroy it. Lot went to seek his sons-in-law, but they would not listen to his words; until at last the angels took Lot and his wife, and two of his daughters by the hand, and they brought them out of the city, saying, "Escape for thy life; look not behind thee." The Lord rained down fire and brimstone, and destroyed the cities, and all that they contained. The wife of Lot was disobedient to the commands of the angel: "she looked back from behind her, and she became a pillar of salt." And Lot was glad to escape with his life, and to dwell in a cave with his two daughters, having lost his flocks, his herds, his possessions, and even his wife.

CHAPTER III.

WHAT HAPPENED TO ISAAC AND TO ISHMAEL.

IN due time Isaac, the child of promise, was born to Abraham, and Sarah was very happy for a time; but again strife and jealousy got into the tent of Abraham, and brought with them sorrow and discomfort. Hagar and her son Ishmael mocked at the young Isaac; and their conduct so angered Sarah, that Abraham was persuaded by her to send them both away; and they would have died of thirst in the wilderness, had not God sent an angel to comfort and help them.

Some time after this, God (who was willing to try the faith of Abraham) ordered him to offer up his son as a burnt sacrifice; and this good man obeyed without a murmur, and had even taken the knife in his hand to slay his

HAGAR AND ISHMAEL SENT AWAY.

son, when an angel stayed his hand, and showed him a ram caught in the bushes, which the happy father offered most gratefully in the stead of his darling son. This was a type of God's love to us. He spared not His own Son, who was also descended from Abraham and Isaac, but suffered him to be sacrificed as a sin-offering for us. How ought we to love and thank God for all His mercies to us! No doubt, Abraham's heart was filled with gratitude, and his tongue with praise, when he was enjoying the company of Isaac in after years.

ABRAHAM ABOUT TO SACRIFICE ISAAC.

We next read of the death of Sarah, who lived to be one hundred and twenty-seven years old; and Abraham bought the field of Machpelah, and laid the body in a cave, that served for a tomb. Abraham was very much grieved to lose his wife, with whom he had lived happily so many years.

Therefore he sent his servant, who was true and faithful to the interests of his master, and desired him to go to Mesopotamia, the country where Abraham had formerly lived, and where several members of his family still dwelt, and to seek for a wife for Isaac. It is true there were young women who lived in Canaan who might have been found, but they did not love and worship God; and Abraham wished to get a pious wife for his son, and not an idolater. Eliezer, the servant, went forth with ten camels laden with provisions and presents, and journeyed many days. One evening, when he had come into the neighborhood where Abraham had directed him to go, he was tired and weary, and sat down beside a well. Ah! my dear children, you who dwell in this pleasant country, where soft mists, and gentle rains, and glittering dew-drops refresh the earth and keep the flowers bright, the leaves green, and the pools and murmuring rills all filled with clear and crystal water, which dances over the smooth pebbles, that purify it as it runs along—you know not how grateful and precious water is in those sandy deserts, scorched by a burning sun, without any grass or weeds, with no overhanging boughs or neatly trimmed hedges to shelter you from its mid-day rays, and where only now and then a cluster of tall, thin palm trees enliven the scene, and are often far from each other; and the only water that can be got is from wells, that are wide apart, and generally covered with a large stone to keep the water from being evaporated (or dried up) by the scorching sun, and sometimes these stones are very heavy, and require strength and exertion to roll them away; and another thing I must explain to you, to make you understand this history clearly—namely, that the greater part of the riches of the people in those days consisted in their flocks.

REBEKAH AND ABRAHAM'S SERVANT.

Tired and weary, Eliezer sat down by the well-side one evening, and having been taught by the example of his master, the faithful Abraham, that God would hear and answer prayer, he prayed to God to send out to him the damsel whom he should appoint to be Isaac's wife. Scarcely had he ended his prayer, when Rebekah, who was a relative of Abraham, came out to draw water. She

STORIES OF ABRAHAM, ISAAC, AND JACOB.

was very sweet and pleasant-looking, and she was also kind-hearted, for she not only gave water to the tired stranger, but also to his camels. And, now that God had answered his prayer, Eliezer made himself known to Rebekah, and presented her with ear-rings and bracelets, and accompanied her to her father's, who gave a willing consent for his daughter to marry Abraham's son. Then Rebekah took leave of her father, her mother, and her brothers, and rode away with Eliezer; and she took with her her nurse, and her maids, and all that belonged to her, and returned, upon the camels, to Hebron, where she was received with great joy by Isaac, and she became his wife; and God blessed them, and twenty years after he gave them two sons, who were named Esau and Jacob.

CHAPTER IV.

THE STORY OF JACOB AND ESAU.

ESAU was wild and high-spirited, and fond of hunting; but Jacob was quiet and gentle, and liked to look after the sheep and goats, and was the favorite child of his mother, Rebekah; while Isaac cared more for his first-born son, Esau: and even at that time it was customary for the first-born son to inherit the most of his father's property as his birthright. One day, when Esau had been out hunting, he returned tired, hot, and hungry, and found his brother eating some red pottage—a sort of stew made of vegetables—and he asked Jacob to give him this pottage to appease his hunger. Jacob asked him to give him his birthright in exchange; and Esau, who was wild and hasty, agreed to do so, almost without a second thought; but the selfish Jacob made him give him a solemn promise, which Esau did, and then sat down to enjoy his pottage.

When Isaac had grown very old and dim-sighted, he feared that he was going to die: so he was anxious to give his son Esau a blessing, and to instal him into his possessions while he was able to do so. He called Esau, and told him to get him some venison, and to dress it, and to bring it to him, that he might bless Esau. So Esau went out into the fields to hunt. Rebekah, who had heard the command of Isaac, called her favorite, Jacob, and desired him to get her two good kids, that she might make savory meat for Isaac, and send it by the hand of Jacob, in order that he might get his father's blessing before Esau returned. There was, however, one difficulty, which was, that Esau was rough, and his skin was very hairy, and the skin of Jacob was smooth and delicate. In order, therefore, to deceive her husband, Rebekah dressed Jacob in the clothing of Esau; she covered the hands and the neck of Jacob with the skins of the kids, so that if Isaac put his own hand upon his son's hand, he might believe that it was really Esau who knelt before him. Jacob, after some demur, agreed to do as his mother advised; she said to Jacob, "Upon me be thy curse, my son;" and this punishment very soon fell upon her, for her dear Jacob was obliged to go away, and I do not think she ever saw her favorite child again. And Jacob, although he succeeded in deceiving his poor, blind father, was obliged to run away into a far country, to save himself from the just anger of his elder brother.

When Isaac smelt the savory smell of the venison, he asked, in surprise, how it was that Esau had found it so soon; and Jacob answered, "Because the Lord thy God brought it to me." Then Isaac, who thought the voice sounded different, asked, saying, "Come and let me feel thee, my son, whether thou be my very son Esau; for," he continued, as he passed his feeble hands over the false skins which covered the hands of Jacob, "the voice is Jacob's voice, but the hands are the hands of Esau;" and before he would eat of the venison, he asked again, "Art thou my very son Esau?" And Jacob, forgetting that God could hear and punish him, and that he could even take away the blessing he was so anxious to gain, answered with an untruth, and said, "I am." Then the deceived father ate the meat and drank the wine which Jacob had brought him, and he kissed and blessed him, saying, "The

Lord give thee of the dew of heaven and the fatness of the earth, and plenty of corn and wine: let people serve thee, and nations bow down to thee: be lord over thy brethren, and let thy mother's sons bow down to thee: cursed be every one that curseth thee, and blessed be every one that blesseth thee." And all these blessings, under the will of God, who had previously ordained and ordered, saying, "The elder shall serve the younger," came to pass, for God greatly increased the possessions and family of Jacob. From him were descended the priests; David, the king of Israel; and, finally, the blessed Jesus, before whom every knee shall bow in heaven and in earth.

But Jacob could not feel happy while his father blessed him: he knew he was doing wrong, to lie and deceive his father, and he was glad to get out of the way before Esau returned. Scarcely had he gone forth, when Esau came in with his venison, and said, "Let my father arise, and eat of his son's venison, that thy soul may bless me." Isaac trembled exceedingly when he heard the words of Esau, and felt that he had been cheated. "Who, and where is he," he cried, "that hath brought me venison before thou camest, and I have blessed him? yea, and he shall be blessed." And Esau, when he heard these words, cried with an exceeding bitter cry, "Bless me, even me also, O my father!"

Then Isaac answered, "Thy brother came with subtlety, and hath taken away thy blessing." Then Esau cried, "Is

STORIES OF ABRAHAM, ISAAC, AND JACOB. 57

ESAU CHEATED OF HIS FATHER'S BLESSING.

he not rightly named Jacob? (which signifies a supplanter) for he hath supplanted me these two times: he took away my birthright, and now he hath taken away my blessing." This was not quite right, because we know that Esau had of his own will sold the birthright to Jacob, and this he could never again obtain; neither could he have the blessing. His sorrow and his tears were unavailing, although he wept bitterly, and cried, "Hast thou but one blessing, oh, my father? bless me, even me, also!" It was too late now. Isaac could not take back that which he had already given; but he tried to comfort Esau by the promise of wealth, and many other good things. Esau was mortified and angry, and he hated his brother so much, that he threatened to kill Jacob as soon as his father should be dead. And this threat being overheard by Rebekah, made her very unhappy and anxious about her favorite child, whom she had advised and led into temptation, and she feared her own act might bring danger upon him, wherefore she now persuaded him to go away from home till his brother's anger should be turned away; and she also persuaded Isaac to let him go and visit her brother, whom she had not seen since the day of her marriage, and Isaac blessed Jacob, and bade him choose one of Laban's daughters for a wife. So Jacob, in obedience to the wishes of his parents, set out on a long journey alone: he had no one to speak to, no place wherein to rest at night. But although God punished him, he did not forsake him: he let him be unhappy for a time, as all sinners must be, unless they repent; and we are taught that "the way of transgressors is hard." After walking all day, until the sun had set, Jacob, tired and weary, lay down upon the cold ground to rest; he put some stones into a heap for a pillow, and fell asleep.

But although he was in a desert place and in darkness,

JACOB'S DREAM

God was with him, and gave him a very happy dream, for he saw in his dream a long ladder, the top of which reached unto heaven, and behold the angels were constantly ascending and descending on it, which he thought was a token that God was watching over and protecting him; and he heard the voice of the Lord himself promising to be his Father and his God, and assuring him that he would go with him, and bless him, and give the whole country round where Jacob was lying to him and to his children, who should be blessed above all the families of the earth. How thankful was Jacob when the Lord promised to be with him, to go with him, and never to leave him until the end was accomplished. When Jacob awoke, he felt very happy. He said, "Surely the Lord is in this place, and I knew it not. How dreadful is this place! it is none other than the house of God; this is the gate of heaven." And Jacob set up a stone there as an altar, and poured oil upon it, and called the name of the place *Bethel*, which signifies "the house of God:" and Jacob vowed there to be his servant, and that he would love him, and give a tithe, or a tenth part of his possessions, to the Lord— which meant, that if he had ten lambs he would offer one of them as a sacrifice. Should not this be a lesson to us, to give cheerfully to our God, and to his poor, a portion of all that we possess? The more we have, the more we should give: and we know that while we trust in the God of Jacob, nothing will really do us evil; even if God should give us trials, as he did to Jacob, he will go with us, and give us blessings in the end, and bring us in peace even unto the gate of heaven.

CHAPTER V.

JACOB IN THE HOUSE OF LABAN.

JACOB'S uncle, Laban, received him very kindly. Laban had only two daughters, and Jacob soon learned to love his cousin Rachel very dearly, and he wished to marry her; so he agreed to serve Laban seven years for Rachel, his younger daughter. And now see the punishment of Jacob: he had himself deceived his old, blind father, and now he is himself to be deceived. Leah, who was the eldest daughter of Laban, also loved her cousin Jacob—she was not handsome, like her sister. So when the seven years were at an end, Jacob asked Laban to give him his beloved Rachel for a wife. Laban pretended to comply, and he made a great feast to keep the wedding. But the bride was veiled, and brought to her husband's tent in the dark, and, lo! when Jacob had lifted the thick veil off his wife's face, behold it was Leah to whom he had been married, and not his darling Rachel: and when Jacob reproached Laban for his deceitful conduct, Laban replied, that it was not the custom of that country to let the younger daughter be married before the elder, and that, if he wished to marry Rachel, he must serve for her seven other years: and Jacob served yet seven years before he could make Rachel his wife.

JACOB EMBRACING HIS COUSIN RACHEL.

It was several years before Rachel had any children, but, in answer to her prayers, God gave her a son, named Joseph. Not long after the birth of this child, Jacob desired to leave Laban, and to go away with his flocks and herds, and his wives and children, and settle somewhere by himself. But Laban persuaded him to stay with him, because he found out that God had made all things to prosper of which Jacob had the charge; and he agreed to give him certain of the sheep, and of the goats, as wages.

Seeing that the flock of his son-in-law was stronger and better than his own, Laban became more and more jealous and selfish, and his sons also murmured against their cousin. So Jacob prayed to God, as we should all do at all times, and more particularly in any time of trouble or perplexity, and God will direct our ways, as he did unto Jacob. "Return," said the Lord, "unto the land of thy kindred, and I will be with thee." So, twenty years after he had fled from the face of his angry brother, lonely and poor, he gathered together his wives, and their children, and their maids, and his cattle, and all his possessions; and he mounted his wives upon camels, and took them all away unknown to Laban. But, three days after, when Laban discovered that Jacob and all his family had departed, he hastened to go after them. But, on the seventh night, just as he had come in sight of the tents where the family of Jacob were abiding, the Lord appeared unto Laban in a dream, and said, "Take heed that thou speak unto Jacob neither good nor bad!"

Laban was afraid to use any violence towards him, whom the Lord guarded. So he spake kindly, and made a covenant with his son-in-law, to be kind to one another in future; and then Laban kissed his daughters and their children, and blessed them, and returned to his own place. And the angels of God were sent to encourage Jacob to proceed on his way.

Then Jacob sent a messenger to tell his brother that

he was coming back, and that he had plenty of oxen and asses, flocks, men-servants, and women-servants, and begging him to be friends with him. He wished Esau to understand that he had wealth enough of his own, without going to be a burden or expense to his brother. When the servants returned, however, they told Jacob that Esau was coming out to meet him, and four hundred men with him. Jacob's heart trembled, fearing Esau would kill him, as he had threatened. We do not read in the Bible that Esau had any unkind intentions towards Jacob; but his own conscience made him afraid. He could not forget that he had deceived and wronged his brother, and that he deserved his anger. But he did the wisest thing it was possible to do—he prayed to God to hear him and to help him. It is conscience that makes us cowards. And, like Jacob, when we are afraid, we should go to God, who alone can protect and help us. God can do good to all who trust in him. And, in answer to Jacob's prayer, God filled the heart of Esau with brotherly love and affection. When he saw Jacob bowing down before him, which he did seven times, Esau ran to meet him and embraced, and fell on his neck and kissed him; and the two brothers wept together for joy. And after they had talked together, and Esau had seen the wives, and children, and possessions of his brother, they blessed each other and parted. Esau returned to Mount Seir, where he dwelt, and Jacob went to Succoth. During the whole night before Jacob met his

JACOB WRESTLING WITH THE ANGEL.

brother Esau, he had spent it in prayer to God. And the Lord sent an angel to wrestle with Jacob, and in the morning, before he would let the angel go, he prevailed upon him to bless him. And as a token that his prayers had prevailed, the Lord changed the name of Jacob to Israel, and from that time the descendants of Jacob are called Israelites.

CHAPTER VI.

JACOB'S LAST YEARS AND DEATH.

JACOB was very happy for a little time after he had made friends with Esau; but soon his family began to follow the example of the people in the land where they were dwelling, and they worshipped idols, and this grieved Jacob, who, at length, by God's direction, brought them to Bethel, the place where he had seen the ladder in his dream, and there he built an altar, and obliged his sons to put away their idols; and because they did not obey, he took away their idols and hid them under a tree. And soon after this, Deborah, the kind nurse of Rachel, died, and Rachel lived but a little while after her. How grieved was Jacob to lose his favorite wife! and what was more sad, she left behind her, besides Joseph, another dear little helpless baby, whom his father called Benjamin. But although the poor mother was buried, and a pillar stood upon her grave, God took care of the little baby, and made his father love him very dearly. Jacob travelled onwards till he came to his father's house, but there was no kind mother to welcome him. Perhaps the sorrow she felt at being parted from her darling son Jacob had shortened her days; and glad as he was to see his father's face once more, Jacob

STORIES OF ABRAHAM, ISAAC, AND JACOB.

JACOB AND ESAU RECONCILED.

must have felt deeply grieved that his mother no longer lived to welcome him, and to hear that his brother had forgiven him. And when Isaac died, at the age of one hundred and eighty years, blessing and forgiving his penitent son, the two brothers buried their father, and wept together for his loss, because death is always sad. We do not like to feel that we shall never see the faces of those we love any more upon earth, even though we hope, for Christ's sake, that we may meet them again in heaven.

Esau again left Jacob, and he and his family, which consisted of twelve sons and one daughter, whose name was Dinah, settled down in the place where Isaac had lived; and Jacob's sons took care of the flocks and herds of their father.

Shall I tell you the names of his twelve sons? They were Reuben, Simeon, Levi, Judah, Dan, Naphtali, Gad, Asher, Issachar, Zebulun, Joseph, and little Benjamin. And you may believe that Jacob loved these two sons more than he did the others, because they were the children of his long-loved, and now buried, Rachel. The favor and kindness that he showed to these children made the other ten sons very jealous, more particularly of Joseph, of whom I shall have a great deal to tell you another time. For the punishment of the fraud and deceit of his early life came again upon Jacob when he was old and feeble. The justice of God thought fit that he who as a son had deceived his father, should be deceived in turn by his own sons; and Jacob's gray hairs were nearly brought with sorrow to the grave by the wickedness and cruelty of his children. But God is merciful; He will not always chide, neither will He keep His anger for ever. He spared Jacob's life until he had been restored to his beloved son, in a distant land. After many years God sent a famine in the land, and Jacob sent his sons to Egypt to buy food, and there, to their great surprise, they found the poor brother whom they had sold, raised by God to be the governor of Egypt. It is a grand story, but a very long one, so that I can now only tell you that Joseph forgave the unkindness of his brothers, and comforted them; and sent for his father and brothers to come and live near him, and gave them a nice place to live in, and a great many good things. What pleasure it was for the poor, old man, who had gone through so many troubles and sorrows, to meet his long-lost son! How they fell on each other's necks, and wept, and thanked God for His many mercies! Jacob was then introduced to Pharaoh, the king of Egypt, who spoke kindly to him, and asked him, "How old art thou?" and Jacob said, "The days of the years of my pilgrimage are an hundred and thirty years: few and evil have the days of the years of my life been, and have not attained unto the days of the years of the life of my fathers:" and Jacob gave unto Pharaoh an old man's blessing. And he lived for seventeen years in the land of Goshen, and he saw and blessed the children of Joseph, and was very happy. But when he fell sick, he sent for Joseph and his sons, and he sat up in bed, and told them all that would happen to them hereafter, and he blessed his own sons, and the sons of Joseph. He told Judah that some of his sons should be kings, and that the Saviour would spring from his line; he also told them that God would keep His promises, and give them the land of

70 HALF HOURS WITH THE BIBLE.

JACOB BEFORE PHARAOH.

Canaan for a possession: and he made them promise to carry his bones, and to bury them, with the bones of Abraham and Isaac, in the cave of Machpelah.

When Jacob had told his wishes to his sons, he lay down in his bed and died, and his soul went to live for ever with God in heaven. Joseph and his brethren mourned bitterly for the death of their father for many days, and then they carried the dead body of Jacob down into Canaan, and buried it with the bones of their fathers—Abraham and Isaac—in the cave of Machpelah.

STORIES OF ABRAHAM, ISAAC, AND JACOB.

His troubles were all over now. Like most of God's people, he had many sorrows, but a great many of these sorrows were occasioned by his own sin. Yet God, who was able to protect Jacob, could also pardon him, and make him happy after death. "Blessed are the dead which die in the Lord."

CHAPTER VII

THE MISFORTUNES OF THE ISRAELITES.

AFTER the Israelites were fairly established in the land of Goshen, they began to look upon it as their proper home, which had been given to them by the permission of Pharaoh, at the request of that wise and good man, Joseph. But as years rolled on, so faded away from the minds of the Egyptians the benefits that faithful ruler had heaped on them. Joseph was dead, and his children; and Pharaoh was dead, and all the people who could remember anything about Joseph. And now a wicked king, also named Pharaoh, reigned over the country of Egypt, where dwelt, in vast numbers, the descendants of Joseph and his brethren, whose story I am now going to tell you. So greatly had they increased and multiplied, that the

Egyptians began to feel afraid of them. They feared lest these Hebrews should rise up and take possession of their country, and drive the Egyptians out, or join their enemies if there should be a war. So they tried to set the mind of their cruel king against the Israelites, and he treated them most unkindly, setting task-masters over them, obliging them to work in the fields, and to make bricks to build two cities, Raamses and Pithom. And the more God prospered the Israelites, the more cruelly they were oppressed by their task-masters, the Egyptians. You may remember that God promised to Abraham that his children should be as the sand for multitude, or as stars in the sky —so numerous that they could not be counted. So, in spite of their hard bondage, the Israelites increased, and waxed very mighty. Then the cruel king Pharaoh, alarmed at their number, commanded that every male child born in Egypt should be drowned in the river Nile, but that the female children should be saved; for he was afraid of the men, but not of the women. You will be glad to hear that certain nurses, whom Pharaoh had ordered to drown the helpless babes, would not obey the cruel command; and God prospered them for their good conduct. And, remembering His promise to bring the Israelites out of the land of bondage to the land which He had promised to their forefathers, God, in His own good time, sent them a leader and a deliverer.

Half Hours with the Bible.

JOSEPH AND HIS BRETHREN.

CHAPTER I.

JOSEPH'S DREAMS.

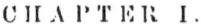

THE Bible contains many beautiful histories; and the one I am about to tell you is among the most touching of all. It is a story about repentance, and kind feeling, and forgiveness of wrong; and tens of thousands of little children have been made better and wiser by hearing the story of "Joseph and his brethren." God, who does nothing without a cause, tells us, in several places in the Bible, that the Scriptures were written that we might learn to be wiser and better. It seems to me that there is a mighty and wonderful charm in this history of Joseph in particular, and I hope, my dear children, it may show you, as it has shown many before you, in the first place, how evil may

THE GOOD SHEPHERD.

be overcome with good, and, in the second place, the BEAUTY OF FORGIVENESS.

The patriarchs, Abraham, Isaac, and Jacob, were shepherds. The shepherds in those days were obliged to watch their flocks by day and by night, for fear of their being devoured by wolves, or bears, or lions. You know who calls himself the Good Shepherd, that careth for his sheep. See how tenderly he nurses the little lambs of his flock!

Among all the sons with whom God had blessed Jacob, the one most dear to him was Joseph; for he was the son of that dear Rachel who had been Jacob's favorite wife, and who, alas! died when her other little son, Benjamin, was born. No wonder, then, that Jacob loved Joseph with a peculiar love, and cherished him more than his other sons; for Joseph must have reminded Jacob of the beloved wife, Rachel, whom he had lost, and buried under the tree; and as yet Benjamin was too young to be much of a companion to his father, though he afterwards loved him dearly. Jacob had made Joseph a coat of many colors, and this kind present raised the envy of Joseph's brothers, who were already jealous of the love Jacob showed to Joseph. What a bad passion is envy! Stifle it, dear children, if ever it rises in your hearts.

It happened that Joseph dreamed a dream; and he told it to his brethren. He said unto them, "I dreamed, and behold, we were binding sheaves in the field; and, lo! my sheaf arose and stood upright; and, behold, your sheaves stood round about, and made obeisance unto my sheaf." And his brethren said to him, "Shalt thou indeed have dominion over us?" And his brethren hated him, and could not speak peaceably unto him. Joseph only told what really appeared to him in his sleep; but his brethren, filled with envy as they were, tried to believe that he

JOSEPH TELLING HIS DREAMS.

wished to lord it over them. Again he dreamed, and told the dream unto his father and his brethren, saying, "Behold, I dreamed that the sun and moon and the eleven stars made obeisance unto me." His father rebuked him, and said unto him, "What is this that thou hast dreamed? Shall I and thy mother and thy brethren indeed come to bow down ourselves to the earth before thee?" For Jacob could not tell the wondrous way in which God intended to lead this his favorite child; and as for his sons, they were furious against Joseph, and hated him yet the more. They gave way to their wicked thoughts, and suffered such sins as jealousy, and envy, and hatred to take possession of them; and, when once these terrible things grow up in our minds, we know not into what sin and misery they may lead us. By envy the brethren of Joseph were led on to commit murder in their hearts. One day their brother Joseph was sent to them in the field, by their father Jacob; and Joseph went to a place called Dothan, where they were feeding their flocks. And when they saw him approach, they were filled with wicked, envious thoughts against the poor lad; and they said one to another, "Behold, this dreamer cometh. Let us slay him, and cast him into some pit, and we will say some evil beast hath devoured him; and we shall see what will become of his dreams." But Reuben, the eldest of the brethren, was not cruel, like the others. He determined to save Joseph from the rest, and to bring him safely back to his father when they were gone; so he said, "Shed no blood, but cast him into the pit that is in the wilderness."

And when Joseph was come to his brethren, they stripped him of his coat of many colors, and took him and cast him into a pit; but the pit was empty; there was no water in it. Reuben, meantime, went away, thinking Joseph was safe; and the rest of the brethren sat down together to eat. While they were thus employed, a company of Ish-

78 HALF HOURS WITH THE BIBLE.

JOSEPH SOLD TO THE ISHMAELITES.

maelites came by on their camels. They were carrying merchandise to a land called Egypt, to sell it there. Seeing this, Judah, another of the brethren, said, "What profit is it if we slay our brother and conceal his blood? Come, let us sell him to the Ishmaelites." And his brethren agreed to this. So they drew Joseph out of the pit, and sold him as a slave to the Ishmaelites, for twenty pieces of silver;—and the Ishmaelites took him away.

When Rueben came back to the pit, and saw that

Joseph was no longer there, he rent his clothes for grief; but the rest of the brethren took Joseph's coat, and killed a kid, and dipped the coat in the blood. And they carried home the coat to their father, and said, "This have we found: know now whether it be thy son's coat or no." And Jacob knew the coat, and said, "It is my son's coat; an evil beast hath devoured him. Joseph is without doubt rent in pieces."

And Jacob rent his clothes, and mourned for his son many days. His sons and daughters tried to comfort him; —but he refused to be comforted, and wept long and bitterly for his son.

CHAPTER II.

JOSEPH'S CAPTIVITY.

MEANWHILE, Joseph was traveling with the Ishmaelites into the land of Egypt; and there he was sold to an officer named Potiphar, who was a captain of the guard to Pharaoh, king of that country; and by Potiphar he was placed as a servant in his house. And the blessing of the Lord was with Joseph; and God made whatever Joseph undertook to prosper.

And Potiphar soon saw what a blessing had come into his house with this servant of the Lord. In time he came to trust and to love Joseph so much that he made him overseer, or steward, of his house, and of all that belonged to him; and so much did he trust to Joseph's honesty, that he did not even take account of his possessions, leaving everything to this faithful servant. And so Joseph grew to be a useful, handsome man.

But the wife of Potiphar was a wicked woman. She tried to tempt Joseph to sin; and, when he refused to listen to her, she was angry, as all bad people are when they cannot persuade the good to join them. She told a wicked lie to Potiphar against Joseph; and Potiphar was very angry when he heard the words of his wife. He believed that Joseph had been unfaithful to him; he never took the trouble to find out the truth, but cast him into prison. Here Joseph remained for some time. But in the dark gloomy prison, as in the rich palace of Potiphar, the Lord was with Joseph. Trust and confidence were inspired, even in that dreadful place, by this good man. God gave Joseph grace and favor in the eyes of the keeper of the prison, who soon loved him, and gave him the charge of the other prisoners.

Dear children, God is everywhere—in the palace or in the prison, on the wild sea and in the deep mine—He is present to watch over those who love and serve Him. He sees every action, and knows every thought of our hearts; and, as he was present with Joseph, alike in the pit, and in Potiphar's house, and in the prison, He will be present with each of you if you truly seek after Him.

CHAPTER III.

THE DREAMS OF PHARAOH'S SERVANTS.

T happened that the chief butler and the chief baker in the house of Pharaoh, king of Egypt, had offended their lord—and he caused them to be put into the same prison where Joseph was; and they were placed, by the captain of the guard, under Joseph's charge. While they were in prison, God caused each of these men to dream a very singular dream. The subject of each man's dream was the same; and they both had this dream on the same night. And when Joseph visited them in the morning, they were both very sad and anxious, because they could not guess the meaning of their dreams. In those days God frequently sent warnings into the minds of people, in the form of dreams. When Joseph came to visit the men in the morning, he noticed how sad these two officers of Pharaoh looked, and he asked them, "Why look ye so sad to-day?" They answered, "Because we have dreamed a dream, and there is no one to interpret (or explain) it." Joseph said to them, "Do not interpretations belong to God? Tell me them, I pray you." The chief butler told

his dream to Joseph, and said, "In my dream, a vine was before me; and the vine had three branches, and put forth blossoms, and the blossoms became ripe grapes. Pharaoh's cup was in my hand; and I pressed the grapes into the cup, and gave the cup to Pharaoh."

And Joseph said, "This is the interpretation. The three branches mean three days. In three days Pharaoh shall restore thee to thy place, and thou shalt deliver Pharaoh's cup into his hand as thou didst when thou wast butler." And Joseph begged the butler to remember him when he was restored to his place, and to tell Pharaoh how Joseph had been stolen away out of the land of the Hebrews, and had done nothing for which they should put him into a dungeon.

Then the chief baker said, "I dreamed I had three baskets on my head, and in the upper basket were bakemeats for Pharaoh; and the birds ate the bakemeats out of the basket."

Joseph said, "The three baskets mean three days. In three days Pharaoh will cause thee to be hanged on a tree; and then the birds shall eat thy flesh."

And the words of Joseph came to pass exactly as he had foretold. The butler was restored to his place, and the baker was hanged. But the ungrateful butler forgot the request of Joseph, who, like himself, had been a captive, separated from his friends; and made no mention to Pharaoh of the prisoner who had interpreted his dream,

JOSEPH WITH PHARAOH'S CHIEF BUTLER AND CHIEF BAKER.

and who was kept wrongfully in the dungeon. But, though the butler forgot Joseph, God did not.

After two full years the Lord caused Pharaoh to dream that he saw seven fat kine feeding in a meadow. And, behold, seven other kine, lean and starved, came up out of the river and devoured the seven well-favored kine. After this Pharaoh awoke, but he fell asleep again; and then he beheld, in a dream, seven very fine ears of corn growing upon one stalk; when, lo! seven thin, shrivelled, empty ears sprang up beside them; and the withered ears of corn devoured the seven full ears that had come up first. Now, these two dreams troubled the mind of the king. No one was found who could tell Pharaoh the meaning of his dreams. But the dreams of Pharaoh brought Joseph to the memory of the chief butler; and he told Pharaoh what had happened to him in the prison, and confessed his ingratitude towards Joseph. Pharaoh sent at once for the young man out of the prison; and, when he had dressed himself neatly, Joseph stood before Pharaoh, and said, "God showeth Pharaoh what he is about to do. The seven good kine are seven years, and the seven good ears are seven years: the dream is one. And the seven thin and ill-favored kine that came up after them are seven years; and the seven empty ears shall be seven years of famine. There shall come seven years of great plenty throughout all the land of Egypt, and after them shall arise seven years of dearth and famine; and the famine shall be so grievous, that the years of plenty shall be forgotten." Joseph then advised Pharaoh to choose some wise man to rule over the land, and to appoint officers under him to lay by in store-houses a fifth part of the great produce of these seven years of plenty, that his people might not perish of hunger during the seven years of want. And when Pharaoh listened to the words of this wise young man, in whom the Spirit of God was, he knew that it would not be easy to find another like him. So, turning to Joseph, he said, "Forasmuch as God hath showed thee all this, thou shalt be over my house, and according to thy word shall my people be ruled. See, I have set thee over all the land of Egypt." And Pharaoh took a ring from his finger and put it upon Joseph's hand; and he caused Joseph to be arrayed in beautiful garments, and put a gold chain round his neck, and gave him one of his best chariots to ride in. And the people were ordered to bow down before Joseph, who was made ruler over all the land of Egypt; and Joseph made laws for the people. He was about thirty years of age when he married Asenath, the daughter of the priest of On. And God blessed Joseph in all that he did, and made him the father of two sons, whom Joseph named Manasseh and Ephraim (which names mean forgetting and fruitful); for Joseph said, "The Lord hath made me *forget* all my toil, and hath made me *fruitful* in the land of my captivity." And Joseph caused the people to fill all the barns and store-houses; and he stored up corn and provisions as the sand of the sea.

CHAPTER IV.

JOSEPH A RULER.

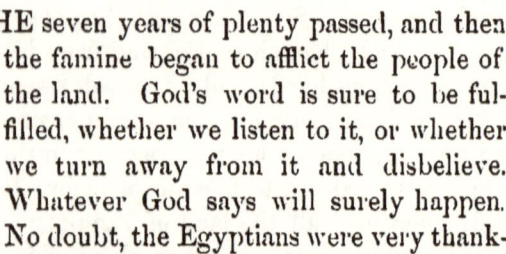
THE seven years of plenty passed, and then the famine began to afflict the people of the land. God's word is sure to be fulfilled, whether we listen to it, or whether we turn away from it and disbelieve. Whatever God says will surely happen. No doubt, the Egyptians were very thankful that Pharaoh had listened to the word of Joseph when he interpreted the king's dream; and Pharaoh must have been thankful that God had raised up this wise and pious man to help them when they were in need. For now the years of famine began to come, as Joseph had said; dearth and scarcity were in all lands, and the people cried unto Pharaoh for bread. And Pharaoh said, "Go unto Joseph; and what he saith to you, do." And Joseph opened the store-houses, and sold corn to the Egyptians; and many other countries sent to Joseph in Egypt to buy corn.

All this time Jacob had been grieving for his dear son, whom he supposed to be dead. He little thought that God had spared Joseph to comfort him and all his family in his old age. And now, when the famine came into the land where Jacob dwelt, there had been no careful governor to lay up corn for the time of scarcity, and Jacob's sons looked at one another in doubt what to do. Then Jacob said to his sons, "Go ye down into Egypt, and buy corn for us, that we may live, and not die;" for Jacob had heard that there was plenty of corn in Egypt.

So Jacob's ten sons went down into Egypt to buy corn. You remember I told you Jacob had another son, the youngest child of his dear wife Rachel. Benjamin was only a baby when his mother died; and, after the loss of Joseph, Jacob could not bear his youngest son to leave him; and he would not send him on the long journey, for he said, "Perhaps some mischief might befall him on the way."

And so, after many years, the brethren who had plotted to slay Joseph stood before him again. He was now a great and powerful man, and a whole nation looked up to him with respect and love, as their deliverer from want and all the horrors of famine. Truly, God had been with him. He knew his brothers when he saw them bowing down before him with their faces to the earth. But they did not recognise their poor, ill-used brother in the fine handsome man who was ruler over the land of Egypt, and who spoke a different language from theirs. Although Joseph remembered his brothers immediately, he behaved like a stranger, and spoke harshly to them; and he questioned them whence they came, and treated them as spies. They solemnly declared the truth to Joseph, assuring him that they were all the sons of one man, driven by necessity to take the long journey into Egypt to purchase food. Joseph felt quite glad when they spoke of their younger brother, whom they had left at home with their father; but he would not show his joy. He told them that he could not believe their story unless their younger brother appeared to prove the truth of their words; and he even caused them to be guarded for three days. And on the third day he went to them, and said, "This do, and live; for I fear God: if ye be true men, let one of your brethren be bound in the house of your prison (meaning, Let him remain here as a surety or hostage in my hands): go ye, carry corn for the famine of your houses: but bring your youngest brother unto me; so shall your words be verified, and ye shall not die." Now Joseph spoke in the Egyptian language, and his words were explained to the brethren by an interpreter. And they, not knowing he could understand their words, said one to another, "This is the punishment of our wickedness, for we were verily guilty concerning our brother Joseph. We saw the anguish of his soul, when he besought us, and we would not hear; therefore is this distress come upon us." And Reuben, the eldest brother, who had interfered to save the life of Joseph when the others would have put him to death, reproached them. "Spake I not unto you," said he, "Do not sin against the child; and ye would not hear? and, no doubt, for this cause his blood is required at our hands." And this is the case with many who do wrong. They forget their evil doings for a time; but when sickness, and trouble, and sorrow come down upon them, they remember the sins of which they have been guilty, and find, in their distress, the just punishment for the wrong they have done. So it was with Joseph's brethren. They mourned aloud for what they had done, and for the evil that could never be undone. They could never make up to their poor father for all the years of grief he had suffered in the loss of Joseph, and they dreaded going to ask him to allow Benjamin to leave his side. Joseph was obliged to turn away to hide the tears that fell from his eyes, when he heard his brother's words. Simeon had been the most cruel among his brethren; therefore Joseph returned and communed with them, and he took Simeon and bound him before their eyes. And he commanded their sacks to be filled with corn, and the money they had brought in payment to be restored to the sacks also; and he let them go.

Greatly were they all astonished when they discovered their money in their sacks. Terrified and anxious, they hastened back to their father, and told him all that had befallen them. Jacob also felt afraid when he saw the bundles of money which they had brought back; and he trembled at the idea of parting with Benjamin, for he said, "Me have ye bereaved of my children: Joseph is not, and Simeon is not, and ye will take Benjamin away. My son shall not go down with you; for his brother is dead, and he is left alone: if mischief befall him by the way in which ye go, then shall ye bring down my gray hairs with sorrow to the grave."

CHAPTER V.

JOSEPH'S REVENGE.

UT the famine was still heavy in the land; and in time they had eaten all the corn they had brought from Egypt. At last Jacob desired them to go down and buy food again in Egypt, for they knew not where else it could be obtained. Then, with great difficulty, Judah prevailed upon his father to intrust Benjamin to his care; and he let them go with a prayer and a blessing, and desired them to carry a present to the ruler of Egypt — "a little balm, honey, spices, myrrh, almonds, and nuts." And he told them to carry double money in their hands, including that which had been returned to the mouth of their sacks. "Peradventure," he said, "it was an oversight." And they went, and again bowed themselves before Joseph, whose heart, no doubt, leaped for joy when he beheld his brother Benjamin with them. He bade the ruler of his house prepare a dinner for them all at noon.

But when the men were brought into Joseph's house, they were afraid, because of the money they had found in their sacks; and they communed with the steward, and assured him that they had only come to buy food, and that they had been alarmed at finding their money

JOSEPH AND HIS BRETHREN.

JOSEPH EMBRACING BENJAMIN.

restored to them. The steward comforted them, and brought out Simeon unto them. Joseph inquired kindly, saying, "Is your father well—the old man of whom ye spake?" He could hardly conceal his joy when they told him Jacob was in good health; and again they bowed down before Joseph, who said to Benjamin, God be gracious unto thee, my son."

But he could not keep from weeping at the sight

of his dear brother's face: so he went into his chamber and wept for joy. And afterwards he made the men sit down to table, while he sat at another table, because the Egyptians were not allowed by their law to eat with the Hebrews; and he sent them messes from his table, giving Benjamin five times as much as he gave the others; and they ate, and drank, and were merry with him. But Joseph wished to make further trial of the good and evil that was in the hearts of his brethren; so he would not make himself known to them, but desired the steward of his house to fill the men's sacks with food, and to put every man's money in his sack's mouth, as he had done before. But now he wanted an excuse to take Benjamin away from them, wherefore he ordered the silver cup from which he was accustomed to drink to be put into Benjamin's sack. So this handsome cup, which was very costly and valuable, was put, by Joseph's orders, into the sack of the youngest brother, and the men were dismissed. But, before they had gone very far on their journey, the sons of Jacob were quite surprised and frightened, when the steward of the ruler overtook them, and said unto them, "Wherefore have ye rewarded evil for good? Is not the cup the one from which my lord is accustomed to drink? Why did ye this thing?" And they replied, "Wherefore saith my lord these words? God forbid that thy servants should do this thing. Behold, the money that we found in our sack's mouths we brought again unto thee out of the land of

Canaan. How, then, should we steal out of thy lord's house silver and gold? With whomsoever it is found, let him die; and we, also, will be my lord's bondmen." And they immediately began to open their sacks, and to search; and the cup was found in Benjamin's sack.

In sorrow and dismay they rent their clothes, and, laying the sacks upon the backs of their asses, they again returned to the city, and hastened to throw themselves at the feet of Joseph. He feigned to be very angry, and said, " What deed is this that ye have done?" And Judah said, " What can we say unto my lord; or how shall we clear ourselves? God is now punishing us for our former sins. Behold, we are my lord's servants; both we and he also with whom the cup is found." But Joseph answered, that he would only take him for his servant in whose sack the cup had been found, and the rest might return in peace to their father. But Judah begged the ruler to allow him to speak, and said, "We have a father, an old man, and a child of his old age, a little one; and his brother is dead, and he alone is left of his mother, and his father loveth him. Therefore," continued Judah, " we cannot go down if our youngest brother be not with us; and, if mischief befall the lad, his father will die, and thy servants shall bring down the gray hairs of our father with sorrow to the grave; for (I) thy servant became surety for the lad unto my father. Now, therefore, I pray thee, let thy servant abide, instead of the lad, a bondman to my lord; and let the lad go with his brethren. For how shall I go up to my father and the lad be not with me? Lest peradventure I see the evil that shall come upon my father." Was this not kind and generous, as well as just, on the part of Judah? He offered to be Joseph's slave, and to live away from his wife and children, and his father, and his brethren, that Benjamin might go back and comfort poor old Jacob. Joseph was touched to the heart; he could no longer refrain from making himself known to his brethren, and embracing them after so many years' absence. So he sent away all his servants and officers, and allowed no one else to be present while he made himself known, for he could not refrain from weeping; indeed, he sobbed aloud, so that the Egyptians and the house of Pharaoh heard him. Then he said to the wondering sons of Jacob, "I am Joseph! Doth my father yet live?" His brethren were very much frightened and troubled at his presence; but he said unto them kindly, "Come near to me, I pray you. I am Joseph your brother, whom ye sold into Egypt. But be not grieved, nor angry with yourselves, that ye sold me hither; for God did send me before you to save your lives by a great deliverance." And he fell upon his brother Benjamin's neck and wept, and Benjamin wept upon his neck. And he kissed all his brethren, and wept upon them, saying, "Hasten, and go tell my father that God hath made me lord of all Egypt, and ye shall tell him of all the glory which ye have seen; and ye shall bring him, and your wives and children, and children's children, and come down, with your flocks and herds; and ye shall dwell in the land of Goshen, and I will nourish you all there; only make haste and bring my father down hither." And again Joseph threw his arms round his brother Benjamin's neck and wept, and Benjamin wept upon his neck; and he kissed all his brethren, and they wept aloud for joy; and then they talked long and happily together. The Egyptians heard what had happened, and went to tell Pharaoh, saying, "Joseph's brethren are come." And it pleased Pharaoh well. He not only rejoiced with Joseph in his joy, but he desired Joseph to say to his brethren that they should lade their beasts and set off at once, and that they should take with them wagons, to bring up their father, and their wives, and all their children, and to take no care for the property they should leave behind them, for that all the good of the land of Egypt should be theirs. And they who had come up to the land of Egypt in fear and sorrow, now returned laden with presents, with changes of raiment, and silver, and food. And Joseph sent to his father Jacob ten asses laden with the good things of Egypt, and ten she asses, laden with corn, and bread, and meat for his father.

The sons of Jacob arrived safely at their journey's end; and they said to their father, "Joseph is yet alive, and he is governor over all the land of Egypt." Then Jacob's heart fainted within him, for he could hardly believe the

DAVID, THE ROYAL PSALMIST

good news. And they told him all the words of Joseph that he had said unto them; and, when he saw the wagons which Joseph had sent to carry him down into Egypt, Jacob's spirit revived again, and he said, "It is enough

Joseph, my son, is yet alive. I will go and see him before I die."

Long after Jacob slept peacefully in his grave, the royal psalmist, King David, sang to his harp of the bounty and mercy of God to his servant Israel and his children; and very grand and beautiful these psalms are. As for Jacob, he hasted to go down into that distant land, and he took with him his children and grand-children—in all, seventy persons. And on the way, at Beersheba, God spoke to Jacob in the night, and promised to be with him in Egypt, and to bring his descendants out from thence, and to make them a great nation. And when Jacob came near to Goshen, he sent Judah forward, to tell Joseph of his arrival.

As soon as Joseph heard the good news, he had his chariot brought out, and went to meet his father; and he fell upon his neck, and wept there for a good while. Oh! the joy of meeting again, after so many long years! The father had grown old and gray; the youthful Joseph, a man of middle age; but they had not forgotten the love of former years. The old man could only exclaim, "Now let me die, since I have seen thy face, because thou art still alive."

CHAPTER VI.

THE END OF JOSEPH'S CAREER.

OSEPH afterwards presented five of his brethren to Pharaoh, and instructed them what to answer when they should be questioned; for the Egyptians looked upon shepherds with contempt, and the family of Jacob had always followed the occupation of shepherds, and he knew that they could not associate with the people of Egypt on that account. So Pharaoh gave them the land of Goshen to dwell in; and when Joseph brought his father before him, Pharaoh asked him, "How old art thou?" And Jacob answered, "The days of the years of my pilgrimage are an hundred and thirty years: few and evil have the days of the years of my life been." By which Jacob meant that he had seen many troubles and sorrows in his life; but yet God had shown him many mercies, even when he thought all things were against him. God was bringing good to pass in His own way; and if we really love God, and are His servants, we shall find that our trials will soon pass away, and that we shall, in the end, have every needful good.

Now, while Jacob and his sons were living in Goshen, and enjoying all they required, there were many poor people dying of hunger in Canaan, and in all the country

JOSEPH AND HIS BRETHREN. 99

JOSEPH MEETING HIS FRIENDS.

around; for the famine was very dreadful, and there was no food for the people, or their sheep, and oxen, and horses. And when these poor people had no more money left to buy food for their cattle, Joseph told them to bring their cattle to him, and he would give them bread in exchange for their horses, or asses, or whatever they might have. And in the next year these poor hungry people had no more flocks and herds to give, so Joseph took their lands in exchange for bread; and thus all the land became Pharaoh's. The next year it came to pass that, when the people had no more land to give—for Joseph had bought all the lands of the Egyptians for Pharaoh—Joseph supplied them with food for themselves and their families, and gave them seed to sow in the fields for Pharaoh, on condition that they became servants, or bondmen, to Pharaoh. "And they said, Thou hast saved our lives: let us find grace in the sight of my lord, and we will be Pharaoh's servants." And Jacob lived in Egypt, in the land of Goshen, for seventeen years. And just before he died, Jacob made his son Joseph promise to him that he would carry him out of Egypt, and bury him in the burying-place of his fathers. And Joseph promised to do so, as Jacob wished.

Soon after this Joseph heard that his father was very ill, and he went immediately, with his two sons, Ephraim and Manasseh, to visit him. And the eyes of Jacob were very dim, so that he could not distinguish them. But when he heard Joseph was come, he sat up in the bed and called all his sons round him, and told them many wonderful things which had happened to him, and of the mercies God had shown him. And he blessed the children of Joseph, and kissed them, saying to Joseph, "I had not thought to see thy face: and, lo! God hath showed me also thy children." Then Joseph bowed down before the old man of one hundred and forty-seven years, and he placed his

JOSEPH AND HIS BRETHREN. 101

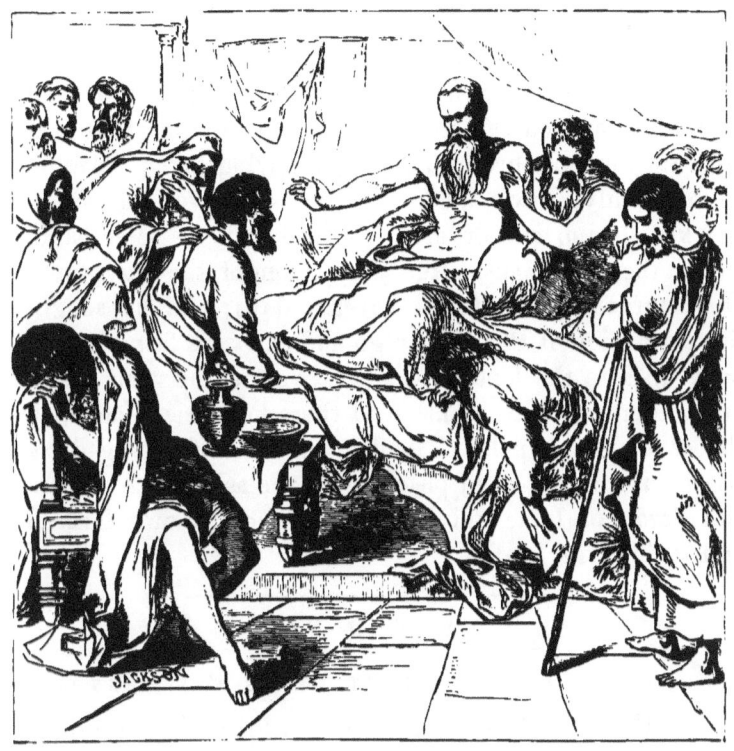

JACOB BLESSING THE SONS OF JOSEPH.

hands upon the heads of Joseph's sons, and blessed them; and he prayed to God to bless them, and make them good and prosperous; and he foretold that the younger son Ephraim should be more fruitful and wealthy than the elder son. He afterwards blessed Joseph, and prayed the mighty God of his fathers to help and to bless Joseph, saying, "By the Almighty, who shall bless thee with blessings of heaven above: they shall be upon the head of Joseph, and on the crown of the head of him that was separate from his brethren." And, having taken leave of all his family, Jacob died. Joseph wept over his father, and kissed him, and ordered his dead body to be embalmed by the physicians, after the custom of the Egyptians. He mourned for his father seventy days; and he sought the permission of Pharaoh to go and carry his father's dead body up into the land of Canaan, whither he went and a great company with him. And there he buried Jacob, in the cave of Machpelah. And so the dust of the aged patriarch rested at last in peace, with the ashes of Abraham and Sarah, of Isaac and Rebekah, and of his own faithful and loving wife Leah.

CHAPTER VII.

JOSEPH'S LAST YEARS AND DEATH.

FTER their return into Egypt, the brothers of Joseph began to be afraid that, now their father was dead, Joseph might be unkind to them, and punish them for their former ill conduct towards him. You see what cowards sin makes of us all. When we have done what we know to be wrong we cannot be happy, even if we escape punishment from man; because God has put into the hearts of all men a feeling called conscience, and this conscience is always troubling the wicked and making them afraid. Very often, they tremble when there is nothing to make them afraid. And now, although Joseph had pardoned them and saved their lives, and made them presents, and been kind to them for seventeen years, his brethren could not forget the evil they had done to him in his youth, so they went and fell down before him, and prayed him to forgive their trespasses against him, reminding him how it had been the wish of their dead father Jacob that they should be forgiven. Joseph answered them with tears of love, and said, with touching humility, "Fear not: for I am in the place of God?" He bade them remember that God had turned the evil they meant against him into good for them all; and not only them, but all the land of Egypt. And he promised to take care of them and their little ones, and comforted them with kind words.

He knew—the gentle, God-fearing man—that to God alone belong vengeance and the repayment of injuries, and that God can take care of His own. Many hundreds of years afterwards, our Lord Jesus Christ said to those who came to hear Him, "If thine enemy hunger, feed him; if he thirst, give him drink; for in so doing thou shalt heap coals of fire on his head." In this spirit had Joseph acted to his brethren. They had treated him as an enemy; he in return fed and cherished them, and opened to them the gates of the land of Goshen, which he gave them for an inheritance; and, with the spirit of a true servant of God, Joseph forgave the iniquity of his brethren, and returned blessings for curses, and good for evil. Should not this be a lesson to us all?

After this Joseph dwelt in Egypt many years. He saw his children, his grandchildren, and their children, growing up around his knees; and, having lived a good and useful life, he made his children promise that, when God should call them up out of Egypt, and give them the land of Canaan, as He had promised to Abraham, to Isaac, and to Jacob, their fathers, they should also carry up his bones with them. Joseph knew that God's promise never fails, and that although many years might pass away first, yet that God would give the Jews the "land of promise." We shall read hereafter how this came to pass. And Joseph died, being an hundred and ten years old; and his body was embalmed, and placed in a coffin; and his soul was at peace with the God he had served so well.

Half Hours with the Bible.

THE HISTORY OF MOSES, AND OF THE WANDERINGS OF THE CHILDREN OF ISRAEL IN THE DESERT.

CHAPTER I.

MOSES' INFANCY AND EARLY LIFE.

A GREAT number of years had passed away since the Israelites settled in Egypt. A wicked king, Pharaoh, sat upon the throne, and he made the Israelites work as bondmen or slaves, and ordered that all their male children should be killed. Then it was that God remembered His promise, and sent a deliverer to His people.

There was a man of the tribe of Levi, named Amram; and he married a woman of the same tribe, whose name was Jochebed; and God gave them a goodly child, a boy. You may fancy what sorrow and distress Jochebed felt when God had made her the mother of this beautiful fair babe. Lest the child should be snatched away from her, she managed, with a mother's love, to keep him hidden three months. Then God put a clever thought into her heart, and she made for Moses a little ark, or cradle, of strong rushes; and she put pitch and clay on the outside to keep the water from getting through. She laid her dear little babe in this cradle, and carried him, with many prayers and tears, and him in the flags on the brink of the river Nile. The merciful God heard her prayers, and preserved the life of the child; for when Pharaoh's daughter came down to wash herself in the river, she saw the ark among the flags, and sent her maid to fetch it. And when she had opened it, she saw the child : and, behold, the babe wept. Then her heart was filled with compassion ; she knew some poor Hebrew mother had hidden her helpless babe there ; and she determined to save its life.

Now, Jochebed had left her daughter near by to watch what would happen to the babe; and the girl went forward, and said to the princess, " Shall I go and call to thee a nurse of the Hebrew women, that she may nurse the child for thee ?" And Pharaoh's daughter said, " Go." Then she went and called Jochebed, and Pharaoh's daughter said, " Take this child away, and nurse it for me." And the woman took the child, and nursed it. The princess called the child **MOSES**; and he throve and grew, and was brought up at the court of **Pharaoh**, as if he had been the princess's own son.

THE HISTORY OF MOSES. 107

MOSES DISCOVERED BY PHARAOH'S DAUGHTER.

But although he was living in splendor and plenty, he was grieved at the bondage of his own countrymen the Hebrews, and angry when he saw the burdens the Egyptians laid upon them.

One day, when he had gone out to his brethren and looked on their burdens, he saw an Egyptian smiting an Hebrew, one of his brethren. He took the Hebrew's part, and in the fight the Egyptian was slain; and Moses hid him in the sand, and thought no one had seen him. But the next day, when he went out, two men of the Hebrews were fighting together; and he said to him that did the wrong, "Why smitest thou thy fellow?" The man replied, "Who made thee a ruler and a judge over us? intendest thou to kill me, as thou killedst the Egyptian?" And Moses was afraid, for he saw that his deed was known. Pharaoh came to hear of it, and was so angry that he sought to slay Moses. So Moses fled into the land of Midian, where he became a shepherd, keeping the flocks of a priest named Jethro; and Jethro gave Zipporah, his daughter, to Moses for a wife.

He often thought of the sorrows of his own people in Egypt. As for the Israelites, they were more unhappy than ever. They sighed and groaned by reason of the bondage, and their cry came up unto God. And God remembered his covenant with Abraham, with Isaac, and with Jacob, and looked graciously down upon their grief.

One day, as Moses sat beside the desert keeping his sheep, he was surprised to see a bush not far off all sparkling with light, as though it were on fire; but, although it appeared to be in flames, the leaves did not fall off, nor was the bush consumed. And the angel of the Lord appeared to him in the midst of the bush;—and Moses said, "I will now turn aside, and see this great sight, why the bush is not burnt." And the Lord called to Moses out of the bush, and said, "Moses, Moses." And he said, "Here am I." Then God told him not to come nearer, but to draw his shoes from off his feet; for the place whereon he stood was holy ground.

When God began to speak, Moses hid his face, for he was afraid. But God spoke only words of comfort to Moses, and told him that He had seen the afflictions of His people, and had heard their cry for help, and that He was now going to deliver them out of Egypt, and bring them into a pleasant land, where there would be plenty of milk and honey. And God said, "Come now, therefore, and I will send thee unto Pharaoh, that thou mayest bring forth my people out of Egypt." Moses was very much afraid when he heard what God intended to do. He knew that he had a very hesitating manner of speaking, and had a difficulty in saying his words, and he tried to make this an excuse for not going. But God promised to be with him, and to help him. And God said, "Go and tell the people that I will deliver them; and tell Pharaoh that if he will not let my people go to sacrifice unto me, I will punish him, and send plagues upon the land." But Moses was still doubtful of his own powers, and unwilling to go. Then God bade him throw the rod he held in his hand upon the ground. He obeyed, and the rod became a serpent; and Moses fled from before it. But God told him to take the serpent by the tail. He did so, and it became a rod in his hand. Then, to give him another proof of his power, God told Moses to put his hand in his bosom; and when he took it out it was covered with a terrible disease called leprosy. He bade him put his hand back into his bosom,—and when Moses drew it out it was cured.

Even these miracles did not convince Moses that he was fit to be God's messenger. So God allowed Moses to take his brother Aaron. When they came to the elders of the Israelites, and told them God's message, the elders were glad and believed, and bowed down their heads and worshipped. So Moses and Aaron went together to Pharaoh, and told him that the great God had commanded him to let the Israelites go, that they might serve Him. But the haughty king answered that he did not know the Lord, neither would he let the people go. And when Moses performed the miracle of changing the rod of Aaron into a serpent, Pharaoh sent for his sorcerers and magicians to turn their rods into serpents; and although God suffered the rods to become serpents, He caused Aaron's rod to swallow up all the rods of the magicians.

Pharaoh was very angry. The usual task of the Hebrews was to make brick, and the taskmasters used to give them straw to put in the bricks, but now, by Pharaoh's orders, the poor people were compelled to go out and find for themselves the straw they required, and yet to produce as many bricks as before. When the people murmured at this cruelty, the taskmasters said, "Ye are idle, ye are idle: therefore ye say, Let us go and

THE HISTORY OF MOSES. 111

HEBREWS AND TASKMASTERS.

do sacrifice to the Lord." So the poor people cried out that Moses and Aaron had set Pharaoh against them, and made their condition worse than before. Then Moses prayed to God for help, and was told what to do.

Early the next day, when Pharaoh went out to the river Nile, God told Moses to go out and meet Pharaoh, and to turn the waters of this beautiful river into blood. And no sooner did Moses stretch out his rod over the river than it was turned into blood; and not only the water of the river, but every pond and stream, and even the water that was in the vessels in the houses of the Egyptians became blood also, and had a horrid smell, so that nobody could drink thereof, and all the fish died. But even this punishment failed to make Pharaoh and his people fear and obey God; therefore He sent a second plague upon them. He ordered Moses to stretch out his hand again over the river after seven days; and there came up such numbers of frogs that they covered the land, and crawled over the tables and into the beds, and even into the ovens of the Egyptians. But now the Egyptians were glad to entreat Moses to ask *his God* to take the frogs away. He listened to their prayers, and immediately all the frogs died.

Pharaoh still continued wicked and disobedient,—and God sent a third plague. He ordered Moses to turn all the dust in the land into lice; and the lice covered the people and the animals. The magicians of Egypt tried to imitate this miracle to deceive the people, but they could not. Then the magicians became alarmed, and they said to Pharaoh, "This is the finger of God." But Pharaoh's heart was hardened, and he would not hearken to them. Wherefore, God sent Moses to meet the king by the side of the river once more, and he bade him say to Pharaoh, "Thus saith the Lord, Let my people go, that they may serve me. Else, if thou wilt not let my people

THE HISTORY OF MOSES.

go, I will send swarms of flies upon thee, and upon thy people; but upon my people in the land of Goshen there shall be no flies."

Pharaoh refused to listen, and very dreadful swarms of stinging flies came and covered the land. Nothing was to be seen for flies; and Pharaoh, in his terror, called for Moses and Aaron, and told them to sacrifice to their God. But they answered that they could not sacrifice to the Lord their God in a heathen land, but they must go three days' journey into the wilderness first. Pharaoh made a half promise that he would let them go a short distance, if the swarms of flies were removed. So Moses entreated the Lord, and He took away every fly out of the land; but, as soon as they were gone, Pharaoh hardened his heart, and would not suffer the Israelites to depart.

CHAPTER II.

GOD'S JUDGMENTS UPON PHARAOH.

THE Lord then sent Pharaoh another message, saying that He would bring a dreadful disease, called a murrain, upon the cattle of Egypt if Pharaoh would not let the children of Israel go. But Pharaoh's heart was hardened. So the cattle, and the horses, and asses, the camels, and the sheep, and all the animals that were useful to the Egyptians, grew sick and died; and of the cattle belonging to the Israelites there died not one. But still Pharaoh remained unmoved. Then Moses took handfuls of ashes out of the furnace, and threw them up towards heaven, at God's command, and they came down as dust upon the people, and upon the beasts that were left, and brought boils and painful sores upon them.

The magicians suffered so much pain from their boils, that they were not able to stand, or to go to Pharaoh when he sent for them. But in spite of all this, he hardened his heart, and would not hearken to the words of the Lord spoken by Moses. The next day God sent a grievous hail, which broke down the trees and all the herbs and plants. Though God had announced by the mouth of Moses what He was about to do, and had ordered the Egyptians to take their few remaining beasts out of the field, some of the wicked Egyptians would not listen. So the hail fell upon them, and killed them. There was hail, and fire mingled with the hail: there had been none like it in all the land of Egypt since it became a nation. But God's people were quite safe. No hail fell near their dwellings, or in the land of Goshen, where they dwelt. No harm came to those who trusted in Him.

Pharaoh still continued disobedient, in spite of the dreadful judgments God had sent upon him; and he offered to let the men of Israel go, but not the women and children, the flocks and the herds; and he drove Moses and Aaron forth from his presence. Then God said unto Moses—"Stretch forth thine hand over the land of Egypt for the locusts, that they may come upon the land of Egypt and eat every herb of the field that the hail hath left."

Locusts are destructive insects, somewhat like grasshoppers in shape. They are very voracious. At last, when they had destroyed all the fruit, every herb and leaf, and every green thing, and the whole land was darkened with these creatures, Pharaoh confessed that he had sinned against the Lord, and against Moses; and Moses and Aaron prayed, and God took away the locusts. But now the ungrateful king again refused to let the people go.

Then the Lord sent a new and a very awful plague upon the land of Egypt: a thick darkness, that lasted for three days. There was no light from the sun or the moon—

116   HALF HOURS WITH THE BIBLE.

not the faintest ray. They saw not one another, nor did they rise from where they sat for three days. But the Israelites had light in their dwellings.

DEATH OF THE FIRST-BORN.

Yet one more plague did God bring upon the Egyptians, and afterwards Pharaoh let them go. But this last plague was tenfold more terrible than any that had preceded it; for it caused one universal cry of desolation to go up from the land, and quelled even the stubborn heart of Pharaoh. This last plague was called the death of the first-born. Moses told his countrymen that the angel of the Lord would pass at midnight over all the houses, and that he would slay the first-born in every Egyptian house, from the first-born of Pharaoh upon the throne, to the first-born of the maid-servant at the mill. God told Moses to instruct the Israelites how they should escape the fate that should befall the Egyptians. They were to take a lamb, without spot or blemish, and kill it in the evening; and they were to sprinkle the blood of the lamb upon the lintel, and upon the two door-posts, that the angel might past over the door when he came forth to slay the Egyptians; and afterwards they were to roast the lamb whole, and to eat it. This lamb was a type of Christ—the Lamb of God—by the shedding of whose blood our sins are forgiven; for he bore the punishment of death, that sinful men might be saved.

And the Israelites listened to Moses, and did as he had told them. They ate their lambs, and packed up their goods ready for a journey; for they had been commanded to get ready for departure. And lo! from all the houses of the Egyptians there arose a dreadful cry of sorrow and mourning; for the destroying angel had killed the first-born in every house, from the eldest son of Pharaoh down to the eldest of the poorest of his subjects. Even the first-born of their cattle died, and there was not a house where there was not one dead. As for Pharaoh, he was so distressed and horrified at this terrible calamity, that he rose up in the night, and called for Moses and Aaron in haste, and cried out, "Rise up, and go all of you, ye children of Israel; take your wives, your children, your flocks and herds, and be gone; and bless me also." The Egyptians, fearing that they should also be dead men, were very anxious to send the Israelites away, and they helped them to pack up their kneading-troughs and their dough, and gave them rich presents to take with them. And thus, in the darkness of the night, this immense multitude of six hundred thousand men, with their wives, and children, and cattle, set forth on their hurried journey out of the land into which they had been brought, only seventy in number, about four hundred years before. God had watched over His people all this time; and though in His wisdom He had suffered sorrow and affliction to come upon them, He had remembered his promises to Abraham, Isaac, and Jacob, and fulfilled these promises by bringing the Israelites out from among their oppressors. How much sorrow and trouble would Pharaoh have avoided had he listened to the words of Moses, and obeyed the commands of God at first! Let this be a lesson to us, not to harden our hearts against God and His words; for He knows all things, and can do all things, and He will punish us if we rebel.

CHAPTER III.

WHAT BEFEL THE ISRAELITES AFTER LEAVING EGYPT.

THOUGH the Israelites were thrust out of Egypt in such haste, they remembered the dying words of Joseph, and they carried out his bones with them to the land of Canaan, whither God had promised to bring them. They went through the wilderness towards the Red Sea, encamping now and then to rest. First they went to a place called Succoth; then they rested at Etham. God had ordered that they should go by this way, and avoid the country of the Philistines, who were strong, and might have attacked them and frightened them back to Egypt; and the Lord went before them by day in a pillar of cloud, to lead them the way, and by night in a pillar of fire, to give them light. Thus they journeyed safe and happy under God's keeping, and following wherever He led, until they came to a narrow pass, called Pi-hahiroth, on the borders of the Red Sea; and they encamped there.

When once the people were gone, the wicked Pharaoh was sorry he had let them go; and he took his horsemen and his chariots, and a great army, to pursue and bring them back. The Israelites saw him coming, and they were sore afraid. They forgot for awhile all the wonders God had wrought in Egypt for their deliverance;—in their fear, they began to blame Moses, and said, "Why hast thou brought us out here to die? It would have been better to stay in Egypt, and serve the Egyptians, than to die in the wilderness."

But Moses said, "Fear ye not, stand still, and see the salvation of the Lord: for the Egyptians ye have seen this day, ye shall see no more for ever; the Lord shall fight for you." And the Lord said unto Moses, "Lift thou up thy rod, and stretch out thine hand over the sea, and divide it: and the children of Israel shall go on dry ground through the midst of the sea. And the Egyptians shall know that I am the Lord." The night was coming on, and while the Israelites rested, the pillar of cloud passed between them and their pursuers, from whom it hid the Israelites entirely; while the side which was turned towards them glowed with light like fire; and all night the two hosts came not near one another. And Moses stretched forth his hand over the sea; and the Lord caused the sea to go back by a strong east wind all that night. In the morning there was a dry path through the midst of the sea; and the Israelites passed through, having a wall of waves on their right hand and on their left. When Pharaoh and his hosts beheld them by the light of day, most of the Israelites had passed through the Red Sea in safety. Then the Lord looked

THE HISTORY OF MOSES. 121

SONG OF MIRIAM.

on Pharaoh and his host through the pillar of cloud; and they were afraid, and would gladly have turned back and fled; but the waters rushed back upon them, and drowned the Egyptians. And the children of Israel saw the Egyptians lying dead upon the shore; not one of them remained alive.

Miriam, the sister of Moses and Aaron, and the women, sang songs of praises for this great deliverance; and all the Israelites danced for joy. They went on their way rejoicing, through the wilderness of Shur; but they found no water until they came to a place called Marah. How glad were they to behold the water; but, alas! it was bitter—too bitter to be fit for drinking. When a difficulty came upon them, the Israelites forgot the mercies they had received at the hand of Moses: they murmured against him, and were discontented and angry. Moses knew where to go in time of trouble; he cried unto God for help, and the Lord, whose ears are open to the prayers of all who call upon him, showed Moses a tree, which Moses cast into the bitter waters, and they were made sweet. Now, you know, the tree of itself could not make the waters sweet, but it was God who gave it such power. He could have made the waters sweet by His word only; but it seems as though He wished the people to see Moses do some action that would make them feel their dependence upon that zealous servant of the Lord, who was to be their ruler and lawgiver for many years. When God had shown Moses how to sweeten the bitter waters, He promised the people that, if they would obey His voice, and hearken to His words, He would not send upon them the plagues and diseases He had sent upon the Egyptians, but would help them.

They went forward and pitched their tents under seventy palm trees, and beside twelve wells of water, at Elim. From Elim the Israelites journeyed to the wilderness

THE HISTORY OF MOSES. 123

GATHERING MANNA.

called Sin; and here a great and pressing trouble came upon them—they wanted bread. Again they murmured at Moses, and wished that they had died in Egypt. Stubborn and unbelieving as they were, they forgot how God had taken care of them day after day; and they regretted the life they had led in Egypt, where, in the midst of their servitude, they had always enough to eat. God, however, forgave their folly, and told them he would rain bread from heaven for them. And behold, the next morning, the earth was covered with a small round thing, as small as hoar-frost; and the children of Israel said to each other, "What is it?" And Moses told them, "That is the bread which your God has sent from heaven for you to eat." They called it Manna, which means, "What is it?" And God fed them with this sweet food, which tasted like wafers made with honey, for forty years. He sent it down fresh every morning, for it would not keep good two days, except upon the Sabbath day; and Moses told the people, on the day before the Sabbath, to gather enough for two days, that they might rest upon the Sabbath day.

It happened not very long after this that the Israelites were distressed for water; not only the men and women, but the cattle, were all fainting for thirst. At once they reproached their kind leader, and were almost ready to stone him to death in their cowardly impatience; and Moses went with their troubles to God. Then God told Moses to strike the hard rock with his rod, and out of the cold dry stone there came a stream of pure water, of which they and their cattle drank, and were refreshed.

Soon after this, they had a battle with a people called the Amalekites; and it was only through the prayers of Moses that the Israelites were victorious. Moses sat on a hill close by, and Aaron and Hur held up the old man's hands, that he might pray for the children of Israel; and the Israelites conquered.

Jethro, the father-in-law of Moses, came to see him, and

THE HISTORY OF MOSES.   125

SMITING THE ROCK.

brought the wife and children of Moses, who had been left with Jethro when Moses went into Egypt. Jethro was concerned when he saw that Moses had to settle every dispute, and to judge every matter among the Israelites; for he saw that the burden of all this work was too great for the undaunted leader, who was now old.

Moses hearkened gladly to the advice of Jethro, who told him to choose out some of the wisest and best of the Israelites, to help him to judge and rule the people.

When they were come to Mount Sinai, God thought fit to give to Moses some written laws for the guidance of this great multitude of people, who were daily falling into some kind of sin; wherefore He called Moses up into the mountain, and told him to let the people prepare for a great solemnity, against the third day.

CHAPTER IV.

THE IDOLATRY OF THE ISRAELITES.

WHEN the third day was come, the Israelites saw a thick black cloud covering the mountain; and out of the cloud came thunder and lightning, and smoke; until the earth shook and the people trembled. They heard the sound of the trumpet, which grew louder and louder; and when Moses spoke to God, the Lord answered him with a voice, and bade Moses go up to him on the mountain; and Moses went up, with Joshua, his servant. And there God spake to Moses, saying, "I am the Lord thy God, which brought thee out of the land of Egypt, out of the house of bondage;" and then he went on to give Moses the ten commandments, which you all know so well that I need not write them down here. And you will think how awful those words must have sounded, when they were spoken by the voice, amidst the thunder and lightning, and the sound of the trumpet! God gave Moses so many other laws, that Moses remained in the mountain forty days and forty nights. While Moses was thus absent, the Israelites fell into very grievous sin. They began to think he would not return; and, with equal disobedience and ingratitude, they went to Aaron and said, "Up, make us gods which shall go before us; for as for this Moses, the man that brought us up out of the land of Egypt, we know not what is become of him. Aaron, instead of telling the people they were wrong, and persuading them to pray and to wait patiently, told them to bring him their golden ear-rings and trinkets; and he broke these to pieces, and melted the gold, and made it into the shape of a calf, after the fashion of one of the Egyptian idols. And then he built up an altar, and put the calf thereon; and they burned offerings before this golden calf, and they ate, and drank, and played before the image, and made merry. They forgot that the Lord could see all they were doing, and how soon they were breaking the promise which they had made.

When Moses and his servant Joshua, who had been with him on the mountain, came down, and heard the singing and the music, and saw the golden calf, and the people singing and dancing before it, Moses was very angry too; he was so wroth that the ungrateful people had so soon forgotten their God and His mercies, and the

MOSES BREAKING THE TABLES OF STONE.

wonders He had done for them, that he cast the tables out of his hands and broke them under the mountain. And Moses said unto Aaron, " What did this people unto thee, that thou has brought so great a sin upon them?" And Aaron tried to excuse himself by saying that the people had compelled him to do what he did.

Moses immediately took the calf and cast it into the fire, and afterwards ground it to powder, and sprinkled the powder on the water, and made the children of Israel drink of it. Then he called out, "Who is on the Lord's side? let him come unto me." And all the tribe of Levi joined him; and he commanded them to put to death a number of the idolaters. And there fell at one time, by the hands of the children of Levi, not less than three thousand men. The idolaters who were spared for a time suffered many plagues and sorrows on account of their golden calf; for, though the Lord protected them, He said, "In the day when I visit, I will visit their sins upon them."

Moses made two great tables of stone, on which the commandments were written; and he abode again in the mountain forty days; and when he came down, his face shone so brightly with the glory of God, that the people could not look upon him, and he was obliged to put on a veil, while he explained to the people the commands of God upon the new tables. He told them that God had commanded him to build a tabernacle, or temple, where His people were to worship the Lord their God. Part of this was to be covered with a veil, and called the "Holy of Holies," in which to keep safely the ark, or beautiful chest, containing the two tables of the law, likewise Aaron's rod, which had brought forth almonds, and also a golded pot, containing some of the manna with which God had fed his people every day. The top of the ark was called the Mercy Seat. It had a golden angel on each side thereof, and their outspread wings covered the top. And the cloud which had gone before the children of

MOSES SHOWING THE TABLES OF STONE TO THE PEOPLE.

Israel rested upon the tabernacle when it was built; and this pillar, which was of cloud by day and of fire by night, stood still when the people were to rest; but, when it moved forward, then they journeyed. And Moses had some beautiful garments made, according to God's orders, for the priests to wear; and he put the garments upon Aaron and upon his sons, and put oil upon their heads, and consecrated them as priests, who were to take charge of the tabernacle, and to offer sacrifices to God.

Moses then taught Aaron and his sons what they must do, and told them what feasts they were to keep. Every seventh year was to be kept something like a Sabbath, and every fiftieth was to be a jubilee, or time of freedom and rejoicing. You would suppose the Israelites were all very thankful to God for these new mercies; but, alas! some of them, instead of being thankful, were discontented and disobedient. Nadab and Abihu, two of Aaron's sons, who were priests, took upon themselves to do what only their father, the high priest, was allowed to do; and they one day put into their censers some strange or unconsecrated fire which the Lord had commanded should not be used. But God was displeased, and sent down fire from heaven and slew them both; and their father and brothers were not allowed to mourn for them. Not very long afterwards, some other Levites, named Korah, Dathan, and Abiram, were envious of the power given by God to Moses and Aaron; and they murmured against them, and said they had as much right as Aaron had to be priests, and to offer sacrifices. Then Moses prayed God to help him; and God, on the next day, told all the people to remove to a great distance from Korah and his friends, and God allowed them to put fire into their censers, and to stand at the door of their tents. And Moses told the people that God would now show them which were the priests that he had chosen, for he would cause all these men and their families to sink down into the earth alive.

And the earth trembled and shook, and opened wide, and swallowed up all these three men, their wives and children, and their tents, and everything that belonged to them; and God sent out a dreadful fire, which burned all those who had encouraged Korah and the others in their rebellion. But although the people were dreadfully frightened at this awful sight, and fled away, yet were they not humbled nor sorry for their sins; but they murmured against Moses and Aaron, and accused them of having killed their friends and companions.

CHAPTER V.

THE LAST ACTS OF MOSES, AND HIS DEATH.

UPON one occasion, both Aaron and Miriam had been jealous of their good brother Moses. They were vexed because they thought God loved and honored Moses more than He honored them; and this was the very sin which had led Cain to murder his innocent and unoffending brother. Therefore, when Miriam and Aaron spoke unkindly to Moses, although he was so meek and gentle that he forgave them, and did not answer their unkind words, yet God could hear them, and He sent a dreadful punishment upon them. He came down in the

THE HISTORY OF MOSES.

SPIES AND GRAPES OF ESCHOL.

pillar of cloud to the door of the tabernacle, and rebuked them for grieving his faithful servant Moses. And the Lord said, "With him will I speak mouth to mouth, and not in dark speeches; wherefore, then, were ye not afraid to speak against my servant Moses?" And when Aaron looked upon Miriam, he saw that God had sent upon her the dreadful disease called leprosy. Then was he sorry for his wickedness, and he knew that he had been equally guilty with Miriam. He begged Moses to pardon him, and to pray to God with him, that God would forgive

Miriam, and heal her of this disease. But Miriam was obliged to be shut up alone for seven days, because she was unclean; and then God healed her.

When the people drew near to Canaan, the Lord told Moses to send twelve men, one from each tribe, to search the land which they were going to possess, according to his promise, and to bring news whether it was fertile or barren, and whether the people who dwelt there were few or many, strong or weak. Joshua, the friend of Moses, and Caleb came back, and brought with them a cluster of grapes, so large that they carried it between them on a staff, and likewise some figs and pomegranates, that the people might see what delicious and fine fruits grew there. But the others came back and said the land was full of giants, and, that although the fruits and corn were good, the people were so numerous they should never be able to conquer them; and only Caleb and Joshua were brave, and remembered how God had always fought for them. The rest began weakly to cry, "Would to God that we had died in Egypt!"

The people of Israel began again to murmur for water, and they reproached Moses and Aaron for bringing them out there to perish with thirst, and they wished they had died with their brethren.

Now comes the saddest part of all this story. Moses—the meek and gentle Moses—who had borne with their ingratitude, and shown the people kindness and forbearance for many long years, became impatient and angry, and both he and Aaron spoke harshly to the people, and called them rebels; and, instead of *speaking* to the rock, as God told him to do, Moses, in his anger, smote it twice

THE HISTORY OF MOSES. 135

DEATH OF AARON.

with his rod, and there came out abundance of water for the Israelites and their cattle. But God was displeased with Moses and with Aaron, and He told them that both had sinned before Him, so they could not enter the promised land; but Moses should be permitted to see it from a distance. Soon after this Aaron died, and after his death the people again murmured. So God sent out fiery serpents to bite the people, and a great number of them died. But Moses prayed to God to spare them; and the Lord told Moses to make a serpent of brass, and set it upon a pole, and Moses did so. And, behold, every one who looked upon the serpent, recovered immediately. Satan is the serpent who bites us, and would kill us with sin, if Jesus, who was lifted up upon the cross for our sakes, did not save us from eternal death and punishment.

Moses was now one hundred and twenty years old; and as the Israelites had wandered about until they were close to Canaan, God told Moses to go to the top of Mount Pisgah, and there He would show the land where His people were to live; and Joshua was to lead, and bring the people into it when Moses was dead. So Moses called all the people together, and spoke to them of the commandments God had given them, and all that He had done for them. And he told them what they must do, and how God would soon bring them into the promised land; and he taught them a beautiful song of praise to God, and he blessed them. And then Moses went up into Mount Nebo, as God had told him to do; and from one of the points of this mountain, called Pisgah, Moses looked down upon the lovely country of Canaan, with its hills and fields, and its vineyards, and so beautifully watered by the river Jordan. Moses could see this good land from one end to the other, and the Lord said unto him, "This is the land which I sware unto Abraham, unto Isaac, and unto Jacob, saying, I will give it unto thy seed: I have caused thee to see it with thine eyes, but thou shalt not go over thither."

"So Moses, the servant of the Lord, died there, in the land of Moab, according to the word of the Lord. And He buried him in a valley in the land of Moab, over against Beth-peor; but no man knoweth of his sepulchre to this day."

Half Hours with the Bible.

THE JUDGES AND MIGHTY MEN OF OLD.

CHAPTER I.

THE HISTORY OF JOSHUA.

MOSES was dead. That true servant of God, so faithful to his trust, so watchful for the Israelites, so zealous for the glory of his Master, had been withdrawn by the command of the Master whom he had served so well. But God did not leave His people desolate. From time to time, as occasion required, He raised up judges and mighty men in Israel, to lead the people against their enemies in time of war, and to judge and rule them in time of peace; and of these judges and mighty men we have now to speak. Each had his appointed work to do, like Moses; but none was so great as that zealous leader, or enjoyed in so high a degree the confidence and favour of the Lord. Yet from the lives of these mighty men we may all learn lessons that we should never forget.

The first of them was Joshua. He had been the friend and servant of Moses; and after the death of Moses, God spake to this Joshua, the son of Nun, saying, "Moses my servant is dead: arise, therefore, go over this Jordan, thou, and all this people, unto the land which I do give to them, even to the children of Israel. Every place that the sole of your foot shall tread upon, that have I given unto you, as I said unto Moses. There shall not any man be able to stand before thee all the days of thy life; as I was with Moses, so I will be with thee: I will not fail thee, nor forsake thee. Be strong and of a good courage; for unto this people shalt thou divide for an inheritance the land, which I sware unto their fathers to give them. Only be thou strong and very courageous, that thou mayest observe to do according to all the law, which Moses my servant commanded thee: turn not from it to the right hand or to the left, that thou mayest prosper whithersoever thou goest. This book of the law shall not depart out of thy mouth; but thou shalt meditate therein day and night, that thou mayest observe to do according to all that is written therein; for then thou shalt make thy way prosperous, and then thou shalt have good success. Have I not commanded thee? Be strong and of a good courage; be not afraid, neither be thou dismayed: for the Lord thy God is with thee whithersoever thou goest."

Then Joshua bade the people remember the promises of God, and the things Moses had commanded them to do. They answered with one accord, "All that thou commandest us we will do, and whithersoever thou sendest us we will go. According as we hearkened unto Moses in all things, so will we hearken unto thee: only the Lord thy God be with thee, as he was with Moses." And God was with Joshua, and did many wonderful things for him. The first of these was the drying up of the river Jordan. Joshua commanded the people to solemnly prepare themselves, and to be ready to follow the ark of the covenant wherever they should see it carried by the priests. This ark was a kind of box made of precious wood, inlaid with pure gold both within and without, and was made by God's order, to contain the two tables of stone, on which Moses had written the commandments; and it also contained Aaron's rod, which had wrought so many miracles for the Israelites, and a small pot of the manna with which the Lord had fed the people in the wilderness.

The people obeyed Joshua; and as soon as the feet of the priests bearing the ark touched the brim of the water of the river Jordan, the waters where driven back, so that the people passed through the river on dry land, quite close to the city of Jericho, which they were then going to conquer: and no sooner had they come into the land, where they could buy corn, than the manna ceased to fall from heaven. And the Lord made Joshua the captain and leader of His people, and instructed him how to conquer Jericho, a great and strong city, with thick high walls.

140 HALF HOURS WITH THE BIBLE.

JOSHUA AND THE ANGEL.

Once an angel appeared to Joshua. It came to pass, as Joshua was by Jericho, that he lifted up his eyes and looked, and behold, there stood a man over against him, with his sword drawn in his hand. And Joshua went unto him, and said unto him, "Art thou for us, or for our adversaries?" And he said, "Nay, but as captain of the host of the Lord am I now come." And Joshua fell on his face to the earth, and did worship.

THE JUDGES AND MIGHTY MEN OF OLD.   141

THE WALLS OF JERICHO FALL DOWN.

Jericho was taken by a miracle. The Priests were commanded to bear the ark round the city once every day. Each priest had a horn; and on the seventh day they all encompassed the city seven times, and Joshua said to the people, "Shout, for the Lord hath given you the city!" And, behold, as the priests blew the trumpets, and the people shouted, the walls of the city fell down flat, so that every man walked straight before him into the city.

CHAPTER II.

JOSHUA'S TRIUMPHS.

THE Israelites were often commanded to put to death the heathen, who were for that express purpose delivered into their hands. When Jericho was taken, only a woman named Rahab, and her family, were saved, because she had before shown kindness to some of the children of Israel. Soon after the taking of Jericho, the Israelites besieged a city called Ai, and, to the surprise of Joshua, the people were smitten by their enemies, for they had sinned against the Lord. Then Joshua prayed to God for help and instruction, and God told him that one of his people had sinned, and He commanded him to draw lots to discover the sinner. So Joshua discovered that a man named Achan had hidden some gold and silver, and a handsome garment, in the earth under his tent; and Joshua brought out the hidden things, and he took Achan, and all his family, and stoned them to death, and burned the bodies and all the possessions of Achan with fire. And after they had done this, the Lord suffered the Israelites to conquer Ai.

You see, nothing can be hidden from the eye of God. He knew who had taken the things, though Joshua did

ACHAN APPREHENDED.

not; and He made the man a public example, to show His abhorrence of sin.

Some of the heathen kings who lived near, combined together to fight against Israel, and they attacked a royal city called Gibeon, with whose people Joshua had made a league; wherefore Joshua and his mighty men went up to fight for them; and God not only suffered Joshua to conquer them with the sword, but he sent down upon them such a dreadful storm of hail, that more men were killed by the hailstones than those that fell in the war. And, in order to show His miraculous power to His people and to their enemies, God told Joshua to command the sun and the moon to stand still. And Joshua said, "Sun, stand thou still upon Gibeon; and thou, Moon, in the valley of Ajalon." And the sun stood still, and the moon stayed, until the people had avenged themselves upon their enemies. Such a miracle as this had never been known before, neither has there ever been such a day since then. The affrighted kings went and hid themselves in a cave at Makedah; and Joshua was told that the men were hidden there, and he caused great stones to be rolled before the mouth of the cave, to keep the kings there until the battle was over; then he had them hanged upon five trees, as an example to others, and he destroyed their cities. Nor did he return to the camp at Gilgal until he had destroyed seven other kings, with all their possessions.

When Joshua had grown very old, God instructed him how to divide the land of Canaan by lot among the children of Israel, according to their tribes; and he set up the Tabernacle at a place called Shiloh, and placed the ark therein. He gave them new laws, and exhorted, threatened, and instructed the people. His last words to the Israelites were very impressive. Among other things, he said:—"Behold, this day I am going the way of all the earth (he meant that he was going to die); and ye know in all your hearts, and in all your souls, that not one thing hath failed of all the good things which the Lord your God spake concerning you: all are come to pass unto you, and not one thing hath failed thereof." And he said, "Now, therefore, fear the Lord, and serve Him in sincerity and in truth; and put away the gods which your fathers served on the other side of the flood and in Egypt; and serve ye the Lord." And, thus exhorting his followers to do their duty, the brave warrior died.

Simeon and Judah were mighty leaders for a time, after the death of Joshua; Othniel and Ehud did some service to their brethren, by subduing the heathen nations, and Shamgar slew six hundred Philistines with an ox goad; and, when they had no other leader, God raised them up a brave defender in the person of Deborah the Prophetess, who judged Israel for some years; and under her rule did Barak lead the Israelites against Jabin and Sisera. Sisera was a Canaanite leader, who was slain by Jael, the wife of Heber the Kenite, in whose tent he had taken refuge after a great battle he had lost; but God delivered him into the hand of a woman, and the Canaanites were entirely subdued. There is a very beautiful song in the Bible, sung by Deborah and the people of Israel after they had subdued their enemies.

CHAPTER III.

GIDEON, AND OTHER MIGHTY LEADERS.

BUT, after all this prosperity, sin crept in among the Israelites, and brought suffering with it. A rest of forty years from war led the people to forget their God, until they were sorely oppressed by the Midianites. Then, in their distress they cried unto the Lord, and He heard them out of His holy hill. He sent an angel to a young man named Gideon. And the angel said unto him, "The Lord is with thee, thou mighty man of valour;" and he commanded him to go forth and smite the Midianites. And when Gideon asked a sign of him, the angel told him to take some kid's flesh and unleavened cakes which he had made, and to lay them upon a rock, and to pour out the broth; and, when he had done so, the angel of the Lord touched them with the end of his staff, and there rose up fire out of the rock and consumed them.

By this miracle Gideon knew that he was indeed called of God to great deeds. So, in the night-time, Gideon took ten men of his servants, and, by the Lord's direction, he cut down the grove, and cast down the altar of Baal, the false god. And when the people saw what Gideon had

THE JUDGES AND MIGHTY MEN OF OLD. 147

THE MIRACLE WITH THE FLEECE.

done by night, they would have put him to death; but Gideon blew a trumpet, and many men were gathered unto him when they found that he was going to save Israel. Then Gideon cried unto the Lord: "If thou wilt save Israel by my hand, as thou hast said, behold I will put a fleece of wool in the floor; and if the dew be in the fleece only, and it be dry upon all the earth beside, then shall I know that thou wilt save Israel by my hand, as thou hast said." And it was so: for he rose up early on the morrow, and wrung the dew out of the fleece, a bowl full of water. Then the brave Gideon knew that he was indeed called of God to deliver Israel. Soon a large army was gathered together: two and twenty thousand men were ready to follow Gideon. The Lord said unto Gideon, "The people that are with thee are too many for me to give the Midianites into their hands, lest Israel vaunt themselves against me, saying, Mine own hand hath saved me. Now, therefore, proclaim in the ears of the people, saying,—Whosoever is fearful and afraid, let him return, and depart early from Mount Gilead." And there returned twenty and two thousand; and there remained ten thousand.

And the Lord said unto Gideon, "The people are yet too many. Bring them down unto the water, and I will try them for thee there." So he brought down the people unto the water. And the Lord said unto Gideon, "Every one that lappeth of the water with his tongue, as a dog lappeth, him shalt thou set by himself; likewise every one that boweth down upon his knees to drink."

And the Lord said unto Gideon, "By the three hundred men that lapped I will save you, and deliver the Midianites into thine hand; and let all the other people go every man unto his place."

Then the Lord told Gideon to take Phurah, his servant, and to go by night to the camp of the Midianites and

THE JUDGES AND MIGHTY MEN OF OLD. 149

GIDEON AND PHURAH.

Amalekites, who lay along in the valley, like grasshoppers for multitude. And Gideon heard one of the men tell another a dream, of which the interpretation or meaning was that God had delivered all the host of Midian into Gideon's hands.

So the three hundred took their victuals and their trumpets; and in each man's hand was an empty pitcher, and a lamp within the pitcher. Then Gideon divided the three hundred into three companies, and desired them to follow him to the camp of the Midianites, and to do exactly as they saw him do.

About the middle of the night, when most of the Midianites were asleep in their tents, Gideon and his followers came suddenly into the camp, and all at once they brake their pitchers, which had each one a lighted lamp in it; and they all blew their trumpets, crying aloud, "THE SWORD OF THE LORD, AND OF GIDEON!" The whole host of the Midianites started up in affright. They cried aloud, and tried to flee. They drew their swords, and, unable in the darkness to distinguish friend from foe, they killed and wounded each other; while those who managed to escape out of the camp were pursued and put to death by the Israelites.

When Gideon and his people were faint and tired with pursuing after their enemies, Gideon begged of the people of Succoth to give them a few loaves of bread for his hungry people, who were yet obliged to pursue Zebah and Zalmunna, kings of Midian, but they refused; wherefore, after he had made an end of slaying the Midianites, Gideon returned, as he had threatened to do, to chastise these churlish men of Succoth; and he punished the elders of the city with briars and thorns, and beat down the tower of Penuel, another city, whose inhabitants had been as unkind to him as the men of Succoth. The Israelites wanted to make Gideon their king. They said, "Rule

GIDEON AND THE ELDERS OF SUCCOTH.

thou over us, and thy son, and thy son's son likewise; for thou hast delivered us from the hand of Midian." But Gideon answered, "I will not rule over you, neither shall my son rule over you. The Lord shall rule over you."

And for forty years there was peace in the land, until Gideon died. But the children of Israel were ungrateful alike to God and to the family of Gideon, their deliverer. This valiant man had no less than seventy-one sons. The name of one was Abimelech. He was a wicked and treacherous man. First, he made a covenant with the Shechemites, and persuaded them that it was good he should rule over them; then he murdered all his brethren, excepting one named Jotham, and made himself a king. But the Shechemites could not love a murderer, and, after awhile, they plotted against him with a man named Gaal, and lay in wait for him to kill him.

Abimelech, having discovered their intention, determined to revenge himself. He went and fought against their city, and took it, and, having killed the inhabitants, he destroyed the city, and sowed the place on which it had stood with salt. The Shechemites who were spared ran and hid themselves in the house of one of their gods: but Abimelech went and set fire to the hold of the house, and burned all the people, about a thousand men, women, and children.

God, in his own good time, punishes wickedness and cruelty; He remembered how Abimelech had slain his brothers, and cut this murderer off in his pride; for Abimelech fought against another strong city, called Thebez, and when he found that a great many of the

THE JUDGES AND MIGHTY MEN OF OLD.   153

JEPHTHAH AND HIS DAUGHTER.

inhabitants had shut themselves up in a strong tower, Abimelech thought to burn them also with fire: but, as he went near to the door of the tower to set it on fire, a certain woman cast down a piece of millstone from the top of the tower, and it fell upon the head of this cruel man. Wounded to the death, he yet called hastily to his armour-bearer, and said, "Draw thy sword and slay me, that men say not of me, A woman slew him." And his armour-bearer thrust him through, and he died. So did God requite him for his wickedness.

Tola and Jair successively judged Israel for about forty-two years, and then the Israelites were once more oppressed by their enemies, until they made Jephthah their captain, and he led them forth to conquer the Ammonites. Jephthah was a great leader of the Israelites, but he is chiefly remarkable for having made a rash vow. He vowed that if God would give him the victory over his enemies, he would offer up as a sacrifice to the Lord the first thing that he should meet at the entrance of his house on his return; and the Lord so willed it that the daughter of Jephthah, his only and much-beloved child, went forth to meet her father, dancing and singing songs of welcome. And when Jephthah saw her he rent his clothes and exclaimed, " Alas, my daughter, thou hast brought me very low; for I have opened my mouth (or solemnly promised) unto the Lord, and I cannot go back." The poor maiden behaved nobly. She said, with pious resignation, " My father, if thou hast opened thy mouth unto the Lord, do to me according to that which hath proceeded out of thy mouth, forasmuch as the Lord hath taken vengeance for thee of thine enemies." And Jephthah was obliged to obey. He was a mighty man; but he could never be a happy man again, and he did not live many years. He had thought himself strong and brave, but God tried his faith, and showed him his weakness.

CHAPTER IV.

THE HISTORY OF SAMSON.

SEVERAL judges governed Israel after the death of Jephthah; but they did evil in the eyes of God, and were oppressed by the Philistines forty years; and then the Lord raised them up a mighty deliverer, named Samson, who was the strongest man that ever lived upon earth. His birth was foretold by an angel, and his parents were instructed by the angel, before his birth, of all that they should do unto him. The first time the angel of the Lord appeared unto the woman she was alone; but the second time, she ran and called Manoah, her husband; and Manoah listened to the words of the angel, and talked with him, and asked him his name. But the angel would not tell his name, and reproved Manoah for asking the secrets of the Lord.

Nevertheless, the Lord accepted the offering which Manoah sacrificed on an altar; and it came to pass, that when the flame of the sacrifice went up towards heaven from the altar, the angel of the Lord ascended to heaven in the flame. Then Manoah and his wife knew that it was an angel who had counselled them what to do. And the child Samson was born, and grew, and the Lord blessed him; and the Spirit of the Lord began to move him. In

SAMSON TEARING THE LION TO PIECES.

one thing he distressed his parents. He desired to marry a beautiful young Philistine, the daughter of their enemies; and when they refused to consent to his wishes, Samson went down himself to Timnath, where the maiden dwelt. On the way he met a young lion, which roared after him; and the spirit of the Lord came mightily upon him, and he rent him as he would have rent a kid, and he had nothing in his hand; but he told not his father and mother. Then he went down and talked with the woman, and she pleased him well. And as he returned, after a time, to take her, he found that a swarm of bees had taken possession of the dead body of the lion which he had killed, and had begun to store their honey there. So Samson took the honey, and did eat of it, and he carried some of it home to his father and his mother; but he did not tell them he had taken the honey from the carcass of the lion.

And Manoah went down, and assisted his son Samson to make a marriage feast at Timnath, and thirty of his companions were there. At the feast, Samson asked them a riddle, which he allowed them seven days to guess: and they agreed to give Samson thirty sheets and thirty changes of garments if they were unable to find out the riddle during the seven days of the feast; but, if any of them should be able to declare the meaning of his riddle, then was Samson to give them thirty sheets and thirty changes of raiment. The riddle which Samson put forth was this:—" Out of the eater came forth meat, and out of the strong came forth sweetness." And three days passed, and none of them could guess the riddle. At length, on the seventh day, they went and threatend the wife of Samson, that unless she would discover for them the meaning of Samson's words, they would burn her and all her family with fire; for they said she had invited them to make a mock of them. She was afraid, and she wept before Samson, and declared that he did not love her, because he had not told her the meaning of the riddle; and Samson said,

"I have not told it to my father and my mother, and shall I tell it to thee?" But at last he suffered himself to be persuaded, and he told her the riddle, and she told it immediately to the Philistines.

So on the seventh day the men of Timnath said unto Samson, "What is sweeter than honey, and what is stronger than a lion?" Samson knew directly by what means they had learned his secret. He went out in anger among the Philistines, and slew thirty men, and he took their garments, and all that belonged to them, and gave the changes of garments to the young men who had expounded the riddle. Then he left them, and went back to his father's house; and his wife was given to one of his companions.

CHAPTER V.

SAMSON'S FEATS OF STRENGTH.

AFTER some time, when his anger was abated, Samson took a young kid as a present, and went to seek his wife. Her father refused to let him see her, and he found she had been given to another, wherefore he determined again to punish the Philistines for their fraud. He went and caught three hundred foxes, and he tied them two together, tail to tail,

THE JUDGES AND MIGHTY MEN OF OLD. 159

with a lighted torch, or firebrand, between them, and he turned them into the corn-fields of the Philistines just at the time of harvest; and the standing corn caught fire wherever the poor frightened animals ran, and the sheaves also took fire, until the flames spread from field to field, and burned all the corn, and the vineyards, and olives. The persons to whom the corn belonged were very angry, and when they found out that Samson had done this unto them because his wife had been give to another man, they burned her and her father with fire. Samson determined to be avenged on them for their cruelty, and as it was God's will that Samson should destroy these wicked people, He endued him with strength; and Samson went forth and slew the Philistines with great slaughter, and took up his abode on the top of a rock, called Etam.

Then the Philistines gathered themselves together, and pitched their tents in Judah. And the men of Judah said, "Why are ye come up against us; and they replied, "To bind Samson, and to do to him as he hath done to us." And three thousand men of Judah went to the top of the rock Etam, and said to Samson, "Knowest thou not that the Philistines are rulers over us?" What is this that thou hast done unto us?" And he said unto them, "As they did unto me, so have I done unto them." Then they said, "We are come to bind thee, that we may deliver thee into the hand of the Philistines." And he said, "Swear unto me that ye will not fall upon me yourselves." They

160 HALF HOURS WITH THE BIBLE.

SAMSON CARRYING AWAY THE GATES OF GAZA.

said, "No; but we will bind thee fast, and deliver thee into their hand." And they bound his arms with two new cords, and brought him from the rock.

So Samson suffered them to bring him bound to Lehi, where the Philistines received their captive with great shouts of joy. Then the Spirit of the Lord came mightily upon him, and he burst the strong ropes off his arms as though they had been flax that was burnt with fire;

and, snatching up the jawbone of an ass that lay near, he rushed upon his enemies, and slew a thousand men therewith. He called the name of the place Ramath-Lehi, which means, "the place of the jawbone."

The Israelites were comforted at the destruction of so many of their oppressors, and they made Samson their judge, and he seems to have judged Israel peaceably for twenty years.

It happened once, that Samson entered the house of a woman who dwelt at Gaza, one of the cities belonging to the enemies of the Israelites; and it was told the Gazites "Samson is come hither." And they compassed him in, and lay in wait all night, in the hope of putting him to death as soon as he tried to pass through their gates in the morning. But Samson was made wise by the Spirit of God, as well as strong; and he lay quiet till midnight, and then arose, and, finding the gates all fastened, he took up the strong heavy gates, bar, posts, and all, and took the whole away upon his shoulders, and carried them and left them standing upon the top of a hill that is before Hebron, so that all might see and know what he had done.

CHAPTER VI.

SAMSON'S FALL AND CAPTIVITY

SAMSON afterwards gave the Philistines an opportunity of getting him into their power. He loved a woman of the valley of Sorek, who was very beautiful; her name was Delilah. And the lords of the Philistines promised to give this woman a great many pieces of money if she would find out where Samson's great strength lay, so that they might bind him and afflict him. And she teased him constantly to inform her where his strength lay, and how he might be taken prisoner and bound. At first he deceived her, and told her if he were bound with seven green withs, or willow branches, that had never been dried, he would be as weak as other men. Then the lords of the Philistines brought her the withs, and she bound him with them, while several of the Philistines lay concealed close by. Then she said, "The Philistines be upon thee, Samson!" But he sprang up and brake the withs, as a thread of tow is broken when it toucheth the fire. At another time, being entreated by her continually to make known the cause of his strength, he told her, "If they bind me fast with new ropes, that have never been used, I shall be weak as another man."

SAMSON SHORN, DELILAH ASKING FORGIVENESS.

And Delilah tried Samson a second time, saying, "The Philistines be upon thee, Samson!" while there were liers-in-wait in the chamber; and again he brake the cords like a thread from off his arms. A third time he made a false answer, and told her that if she would weave seven locks of his hair with a weaver's beam, and fasten it with the pin of the beam, he would become powerless. And she did so, while Samson was asleep; but when she told him the Philistines were at hand, he waked up and went away

SAMSON BOUND.

with the pin of the beam and with the web. At last Delilah said, "How canst thou say, I love thee, when thine heart is not with me? Thou hast mocked me these three times, and hast not told me wherein thy great strength lieth." And she pressed him daily with her words, and urged him, so that his soul was vexed to death, till at last he opened his heart to her, and told this wicked woman the secret—that he had never had a razor upon his head; and that, if he were shaven, all his strength would depart from him, for he would no longer be a Nazarite, or holy man, to the Lord. Delilah knew that he had spoken truth. And she called the lords of the Philistines, and told them all that Samson had said; and one day, when she had persuaded Samson to lie down and sleep, she called the Philistines, who brought with them the money they had promised to Delilah. And when the seven locks had been cut from Samson's head, the Philistines sprang on him, and put out his eyes. Then they took him down to Gaza, and bound him with fetters of brass, and made him grind in the prison-house. So now he was obliged to work like a slave for the enemies who had so feared him. No doubt he often repented for his wickedness, and called upon God to help him in his trouble; and so, as his hair grew again, God imparted to him his former strength.

CHAPTER VII.

THE DEATH OF SAMSON.

THE Philistines rejoiced greatly at the capture of Samson. They determined to make the offering of a sacrifice to Dagon, one of their gods; for they believed that it was Dagon who had delivered Samson into their hands. When the people saw him, they praised their god for delivering Samson into their hands.

Then they sent for the poor blind prisoner, to make sport for them in the temple of the house of Dagon.

He was brought out of the prison, and they placed him between the strong pillars that supported the roof, and he was compelled to make sport for them. Then Samson took hold of the pillars with his hands; and he prayed to the Lord, saying, " O Lord God, remember me, I pray thee, and strengthen me, I pray thee, only this once, O God, that I may be at once avenged of the Philistines for my two eyes." And taking the two pillars, one with his right hand and the other with his left, he bowed himself with all his might, and pulled down the whole house, and killed all the thousands of Philistines that it contained. Samson was killed himself. He knew that this must be the case, but he felt that he destroyed more people at his death than he had done while living. It was a sad death for him to die; but, you see, when he forgot the Lord, and the Lord's people, the Lord forsook Samson, or, rather, suffered him to bring upon himself his own punishment.

The death of Samson left the Israelites without a leader, and every one did as he pleased. All was trouble and confusion, until God raised up to them a righteous judge, called Samuel. God gave this child Samuel to a good woman, named Hannah, in answer to her prayer. He was brought up with the high priest, Eli, in the temple, and was called by God to be a prophet in his early childhood.

THE JUDGES AND MIGHTY MEN OF OLD.   167

SAMSON PULLING DOWN THE TEMPLE OF DAGON.

And after the death of Eli and his sons, Samuel judged Israel, and helped the people to overcome their enemies, the Philistines; for, in answer to the prayer of Samuel, God sent thunder upon the Philistines, and so discomfited them that they were smitten before Israel. And Samuel judged Israel righteously for many years, but his sons took bribes from the people, and were selfish, and fond of money and pleasure; so that the Israelites were discontented, and murmured, and besought Samuel to give them a king.

Samuel warned them that any other king but God would bring much trouble upon them, but they would not hearken; wherefore God suffered them to have a king, and told Samuel whom he should anoint to be their king. And Samuel made Saul king over Israel; and although he was then very old, he lived to see the troubles he had foretold brought upon the Israelites—he lived to see Saul rejected by the Lord, and to mourn over his sin.

He was afterwards employed by the Lord to anoint David, the son of Jesse, to be king over the Israelites in the stead of Saul; but he was not spared to see David upon the throne of Israel. He died at a great age, before Saul perished miserably in battle; and all the Israelites gathered together and buried Samuel at Ramah, where he had lived; and they mourned for this good man, who was one of the best, as he was the last, of the judges of Israel. But it was not his valour, as with Joshua and Gideon, nor his strength, as with Samson, but his justice and love of God, that made him honoured and esteemed by his people. By faith all these mighty men subdued kingdoms and wrought righteousness, for it was with the greatest of them as with the least: so long as they wrought in the strength of God, and for His glory, they were prosperous and mighty; when they became cruel like Abimelech, or foolish like Samson, or careless like Eli, their strength was turned to weakness, and they were compelled to confess that it is the Lord who setteth up and who casteth down.

Half Hours with the Bible.

THE KINGS OF ISRAEL AND JUDAH.

CHAPTER I.

HOW THE KINGS CAME TO BE CHOSEN.

IT is an evil thing for a country when there is no just judge—no one to see that the laws are kept, to prevent the rich from oppressing the poor, and the poor from being idle and dishonest, and the evil-doer from troubling the just; and so it was in Israel at the time of which I have to speak. Every man did what was right in his own eyes. The Israelites, who had now settled down in the promised land, were surrounded by heathen enemies, and some of their judges were not wise and equitable men. While the good Samuel swayed the scale of justice, they were contented, and might have been happy, for they had

God for their king. But they became discontented, and importuned Samuel, with many words, to give them a king. The Lord told Samuel to protest solemnly to the people, and to show them the manner of king that should reign; to tell them that the king would tax them and oppress them, and make them fight his battles, and use them as slaves, if they determined to elect one. And when they would not listen, but persisted in having a king who might lead them to battle, God ordered Samuel to anoint a king over them. Under God's direction, there came to Samuel a young, tall, handsome man, of the tribe of Benjamin; his name was Saul. Saul came to Samuel for advice. And the Lord said unto Samuel, "Behold, this is the man that thou shalt anoint to be king over Israel." So, after some conversation, Samuel poured a vial of oil upon his head, and kissed him, and said to him, "The Lord hath anointed thee to be king over his inheritance;" and God blessed Saul, and sent His spirit upon him, so that Saul was enabled to prophesy. And soon after this, Samuel brought Saul and set him before the people; and the people saw that Saul was taller by the head and shoulders than the rest of the people; and they shouted and cried, "God save the king!"

Most of the people were delighted with their king, and a select company followed and remained with Saul. But there were a few jealous, envious people, who despis-

DAVID PLAYING BEFORE SAUL.

ed Saul, and said, "How shall this man save us from our enemies?" He soon proved his bravery, however; for the Ammonites besieged the people of Jabesh-Gillead, his neighbors, and Saul, hearing of their distress, gathered an army, and defeated the Ammonites, and put them to flight. The people, overjoyed with their conquest, wished to put to death the ungrateful men who had despised their king; but Saul said, "There shall not a man be put to death this day, for to-day God hath wrought salvation in Israel." And the people followed Saul to Gilgal, and there they offered peace offerings before the Lord; and Saul, and all the men of Israel, rejoiced greatly.

Soon after this, Saul was sent to execute judgment upon the Amalekites, and God, being justly displeased with this heathen nation, had ordered Saul to put every living thing, man and woman, child, and four-footed beast, to the sword. Saul, however, again disobeyed his Heavenly King, and saved the king, Agag, and the finest of the cattle and sheep. But when Samuel came, Saul first wanted him to believe that he had fulfilled the command of the Lord. Samuel asked, "What meaneth, then, this bleating of the sheep in mine ears, and this lowing of the oxen that I hear?" Saul then wished to excuse himself, and pretended he had spared the cattle for sacrifice. But Samuel made this solemn and impressive answer;— "Hath the Lord as great delight in burnt offerings and sacrifices as in obeying the voice of the Lord? Behold, to obey is better than sacrifice, and to harken than the fat of rams. For rebellion is as the sin of witchcraft, and stubborness is as iniquity and idolatry. Because thou hast rejected the word of the Lord, He also hath rejected thee from being king." And Saul said unto Samuel, "I have sinned, for I have transgressed the commandment of the Lord and his words; because I feared the people, and obeyed their voice. Now, therefore, I pray thee, pardon my sin, and turn again with me, that I may worship the Lord." But Samuel said, "The Lord hath rent the kingdom of Israel from thee this day, and hath given it to a neighbour of thine, who is better than thou." And Samuel with his own hand carried out the sentence that the Lord had pronounced against Agag, king of the Amalekites.

Samuel came no more to see Saul to the day of his death. Nevertheless Samuel mourned for Saul. And the spirit of the Lord departed from Saul, and an evil spirit troubled him. He could not even sleep in peace. So some of his friends brought before him a young shepherd lad, named David, who was skilled in playing the harp, and they hoped that his sweet music might divert the mind of the unhappy king. And Saul sent messengers to Jesse, David's father, requesting that David might remain with him, for he found favor in Saul's sight. And when David took his harp and played, the evil spirit departed from Saul.

CHAPTER II.

DAVID'S EARLY EXPLOITS.

NOT only was David a clever musician, but he was very brave, although he was so young. One day, when he was keeping his father's sheep, there came a lion and a bear to steal the sheep; but by the help of God, David slew both these fierce and strong animals, without any other assistance. And when God suffered the Philistines, with a great giant at their head, to go and terrify Saul and his people with their threats, God put it into the heart of the young shepherd to go forth and meet this strong and warlike giant, who was armed with a sword and a spear. David, however, took only a sling, which is a slip of leather, and a few stones in his hand; and, while the huge giant, Goliath, was threatening to kill David, and give his flesh to the fowls of the air, David put a stone into his sling, and let it fly; and the stone hit the giant on the forehead, and sank into his head, so that Goliath fell dead upon the ground. Then David cut off the head of the giant, and the terrified Philistines fled. But the Israelites, when they saw the giant was dead, followed after their enemies, and put numbers of them to death, and then returned and plundered the tents of the

THE KINGS OF ISRAEL AND JUDAH. 175

DAVID AND GOLIATH.

Philistines. And the people sang a fine song in praise of David and his bravery, saying, "Saul hath slain his thousands, and David his ten thousands." Now this made Saul very jealous—that to him should be ascribed thousands only, and to David tens of thousands; and, forgetting the great service David had done for Israel, he tried on several occasions to kill the youth. But God preserved David's life, although once he was obliged to pretend to be mad, and had to hide himself in a cave, and Saul hunted to and fro after him.

DAVID TAKES SAUL'S SPEAR.

While David was roaming about in fear of Saul, he once sent to a rich man named Nabal, and begged that he would supply him and his followers with some food; but Nabal was covetous, and would not give them so much as a drop of water. This man had a beautiful young wife, named Abigail; she was sorry when she heard what her husband had done, and she immediately took some wine, and bread, and fruits, and herself carried the provisions to David. God punished Nabal for his greediness by death, and David afterwards married Abigail.

THE KINGS OF ISRAEL AND JUDAH. 177

Saul had promised to give his daughter Michal, as a wife, to whosoever should kill the giant; and Michal and her brother Jonathan, Saul's son, loved David very dearly, and they both helped to save David from the fury of their father; and David again spared the life of Saul, when he was marching about to slay him. But God punished Saul for his cruelty by means of the Philistines, who harassed and distressed the kingdom. At last there was a terrible battle, at Gilboa, in which Jonathan and two other sons of Saul were killed; and Saul, in his despair, killed himself.

CHAPTER III.

DAVID'S LATER DAYS, AND THE STORY OF SOLOMON.

DAVID grieved very much for Jonathan, although he was now made King of Judah. For a short time the other tribes claimed Ishbosheth, a son of Saul, for their king; but Ishbosheth was murdered by his own captains, and David was king over the twelve tribes. As soon as he was peaceably settled in his kingdom, David wished to build a temple to the Lord, but God only allowed David to get the materials ready for the building, because he had been a man of war. And David showed great kindness to all the descendants of Jonathan, for his friend's sake. But now that David was happy and in high station, he fell into temptation, and sinned against God; he wished to marry Bathsheba, the wife of Uriah, one of his captains; and, because he wished to have her for a wife, David sent Uriah, her husband, out into the battle, and had the poor man placed in front of the battle, so that he was killed: and then David took Bathsheba as his wife. The Lord was greatly angered, and He sent the prophet Nathan to show David the wickedness of his conduct, and to reprove him for it; and He moreover, smote with sickness the poor little child who had been born to David, so that it died. And David mourned, and prayed to God in vain to spare its life. Thus God punished the father by the death of his child; and, all through the remainder of David's days, God suffered the sons of David to cause sorrow to their father by deeds of blood.

One of his sons, a very handsome youth, named Absalom, rebelled against his father, collected an army and fought against David, and drove him away from Jerusalem, and tried to make himself king in his father's stead; but after a time, his army was conquered by the army of David; and, as he tried to ride quickly away, to hide himself in a wood, Absalom's long, beautiful hair, of which he had been very proud, caught in the boughs of an oak tree, and he was dragged off his mule, and hung suspended in the air, until one of the king's officers, a captain

THE DEATH OF ABSALOM.

named Joab, went and put him to death. But David mourned for Absalom very bitterly.

David died when he was about seventy years of age, and left his kingdom, and much good advice, to his son Solomon, who was the wisest among all the kings who reigned over Israel.

Solomon was at first opposed by Adonijah, one of the sons of David, who wished to make himself king by the help of Joab, captain of the host, and Abiathar, the priest.

DAVID'S PARTING ADVICE

But Adonijah and Joab were put to death, and Abiathar was deprived of his office. Then Solomon took possession of his kingdom. He at once gave all his attention to the building of a beautiful temple, in which to worship the Lord, for he loved God; and, in a vision, he asked of the Lord wisdom, in preference to long life, honor, or riches. One of the wise judgments of Solomon has been recorded for our instruction. The matter was this:—Two women came before his throne, and one of them said, "O king, this woman and I dwelt in the same house, and each of us had a babe three days old. In the night, her child died; and she rose at midnight, while I was asleep, and took away my living child, and laid her dead child in my arms." And the other woman said, "Nay; but the living son is mine, and the dead son is hers." Now Solomon knew that the real mother would not allow any harm to come to her child; so he said, "Bring me a sword;" and they brought a sword. Then he said, "Divide the living child in two; and give the half to one, and the half to the other." Then the woman to whom the child belonged cried out, "O, my lord, give her the child, and in no wise slay it!" But the other said, "Divide it!" Then Solomon gave the child to the woman who had compassion on it.

When the temple was finished, it exceeded in beauty all the buildings of the earth; and, when the ark was placed therein by the priests, the glory of the Lord filled the house. Solomon offered a very devout prayer to God, begging him to hear the prayers that should be offered in the temple, and to avert all evil, and to forgive all the faults of His people, and their shortcomings, when they cried to Him for pardon. And the fame of Solomon's temple, and of his house, his riches, and his wisdom, went over all the earth. The Queen of Sheba travelled from her own distant country to see and hear the wisdom of Solomon, and she tried him with hard questions, but he answered them all. But, alas! in his old age Solomon

THE JUDGMENT OF SOLOMON.

forgot all that God had given to him and done for him. He fell into sin, and suffered his heathen wives to lead him into idolatry; and, to please them, he built temples for the worship of idols. Justly was God displeased with him, and He threatened Solomon that he would take away a great portion of the kingdom from his son, on account of Solomon's wickedness. And Solomon died, after he had reigned forty years over Israel.

CHAPTER IV.

SOLOMON'S SUCCESSORS.

REHOBOAM, the son of Solomon, was made king after the death of his father. His conduct soon gave offence to many of the old and wise counsellors who had helped his father to govern. He scorned their good advice, and threatened to increase the burdens of the people. He said, " Whereas my father did lade you with a heavy yoke, I will add to your yoke. My father hath chastised you with whips, but I will chastise you with scorpions." Ten of the tribes of Israel were so much offended that they threw off his yoke, and made Jeroboam, a bold, ambitious youth, their king. There were now two distinct kingdoms. One was called Israel, and the other, which consisted only of the tribes of Judah and Benjamin, was called the kingdom of Judah. Of this latter kingdom, Jerusalem, with its beautiful temple, was the capital. Sometimes there was war between these two kingdoms. Rehoboam raised an army of an hundred and eighty thousand chosen men, and wished to make war upon the Israelites; but Shemaiah, the prophet, brought him a message from the Lord, forbidding him to go to war; and Rehoboam and his men hearkened to the word of the Lord, and gave up their design. The king, however, gave himself up to his idle companions, to wickedness, and idolatry, until the Lord, in His anger, permitted the Egyptians to enter Jerusalem, and to take away the treasures out of the temple and out of the king's house. Rehoboam reigned seventeen years. After his death, Abijam, his son, became king, and he at once went to war against Jeroboam; and he recovered many cities and strong places from the Israelites. Yet the Bible tells that Abijam walked in the sins of his father, Rehoboam, and that his heart was not perfect with the Lord.

He was succeeded by his son Asa, who began his reign well, by serving the Lord. He removed the idols and their temples out of his kingdom, and banished many persons who did evil. He even banished his own mother, Maachah, from the palace, where she had reigned as queen, because she had broken the commandments, and made an idol, to which she bowed down; and Asa destroyed her idol, and burnt it by the brook Kidron.

Jehoshaphat, Asa's son, the next king, entirely destroyed the idolators and their idols, and sent holy men to instruct his subjects in their duty to God. His own people loved their good king, and the neighboring nations honored him; but he suffered his son to marry the daughter of an idolator, and he foolishly made a league with the King of Syria, who was also an idolator; and God, to show his displeasure, suffered the Moabites and Ammonites to invade Jehoshaphat's dominions; and, upon his repentance, the Lord deceived the heathen armies, so that they killed each other in their dismay; and Jehoshaphat ended his reign in peace.

After the death of Jehoshaphat, Jehoram became king, and, under the influence of his wicked wife, he murdered all his own brothers, and then worshipped Baal, and other idols, as she did. The Lord punished his idolatry by suffering the Edomites, Philistines, and Ammonites to invade the country and plunder Jerusalem, and he died miserably of a very painful disorder.

Ahaziah, his son, made a friendship with Jehoram, king of Israel, and went with him to fight against Jehu, the son of Jehoshaphat, whom the Lord had chosen to rule over Israel; and both were killed in the battle. After his death, his wicked mother, Queen Athaliah, put most of her grandchildren to death, and made herself governor of the kingdom. Joash, the youngest son, was, however, secretly saved, and hidden, with his nurse, in the temple for six years. Then the high priest and others placed Joash on the throne, and the people cried "God save the king!" Then the wicked queen Athaliah was in her turn murdered. So long as Joash continued under the care and advice of Jehoiada, the good priest, he was pious and amiable, but as soon as Jehoiada died, and Joash was left to himself, he forsook God, and began to follow idols; and, forgetting all the kindness he owed to the good Jehoiada, he was so ungrateful as to put his son to death, because he had reproved the king for his wickedness. The Lord then suffered great troubles and diseases to fall upon Joash; He permitted the Syrians to spoil his country, and to carry away his treasures, and to slay his subjects; and, last of all, his own servants conspired against the unhappy king, and they murdered him in his bed.

Amaziah, his son, was struck by the solemn judgments that had happened to Joash, and he began his reign with piety and moderation. He was successful in his battles with the neighboring nations. But these victories filled his heart with pride, and he began to worship idols. He was defeated by the king of Israel. His own subjects conspired against him, and he fled away from Jerusalem; but they followed after him, and slew him at **Lachish**.

CHAPTER V.

KINGS OF JUDAH.

UZZIAH, also called Azariah, succeeded to the throne of Judah. He, too, began his reign well; he was wise and good, and the land prospered under his rule. But it was with him as with almost every one of these kings. When he was full, he forgot the Giver, and became puffed up with pride, and took upon himself the office of a priest; but when he attempted to burn incense to the Lord, he was struck with a dreadful disease called leprosy, so that he was obliged to leave his throne, and hide himself from his subjects for the rest of his days. How many lessons we may learn from God's dealings with his ancient people! How ought we to strive to avoid the feelings of pride and other faults, which brought such heavy punishment upon them! Let us say with all our hearts—"Lead us not into temptation."

When Uzziah was thus unable to attend to his affairs, his son Jotham took the government into his hands. He was a good youth, and reigned with greater wisdom than his father; but after his death, Ahaz his son reigned over Judah, and Ahaz was an idolator, and a wickeder man than any who had reigned over Judah. He not only sacrificed to heathen gods, but he went so far as to shut up

188 HALF HOURS WITH THE BIBLE.

ISAIAH BEFORE HEZEKIAH.

the doors of the temple of the Lord. His kingdom was invaded by the Syrians, and the Israelites his people were carried away captives; until the Lord put an end to the wickedness of Ahaz by cutting him off in his youth. His son, Hezekiah, did all he could to remedy the distresses of his country as soon as he became king; he destroyed the idols and their temples, opened the holy temple, and encouraged the priests and people to worship the Lord God Almighty, and he offered burnt offerings and sang praises to God. He sent letters to the Israelites, as well as to his own subjects, inviting them to attend the services in the temple and to keep the feast.

Being seized with a painful disorder, he was visited by the prophet Isaiah, who told him to set his house in order because he must die. Hezekiah was much distressed to hear this message; he grieved that he must die and leave his country to the Assyrians, who were then invading it; and he prayed earnestly to God that he might be spared a little longer. The merciful Lord hearkened to his prayer, and spared his life for fifteen years longer. But before this sickness befell him, Hezekiah had received an infamous letter from Sennacherib, king of Assyria, threatening to destroy Jerusalem. Hezekiah, trusting in the Lord's promise, prepared for the defence, and the Lord promised him help by the mouth of Isaiah the prophet; and during the night the Lord sent an angel and smote all the Assyrians, and when Hezekiah and his people arose in the morning, the city was surrounded with the dead bodies of their enemies. Although the Assyrian king, Sennacherib, escaped for a while, he was soon after killed by his own sons. After this, Hezekiah increased in honor and riches, and had many treasures; but, when the king of Babylon sent him a present, he was vain enough to expose all his possessions to the messengers, and Isaiah was sent by God to reprove him for his folly, and to tell him that all these things would be hereafter carried away to Babylon, where Hezekiah's descendants should be slaves in the king's palace.

Hezekiah ended his life in peace, and left the crown to his son Manasseh. Manasseh was twelve years old when he began to reign, and he reigned fifty-five years in Jerusalem; and he did that which was wicked in the sight of the Lord, and abandoned himself to the worship of idols. He went on from one wickedness to another, putting the Lord's prophets to death, and we are told that he seduced the people to do more wickedness than those nations whom the Lord destroyed before the children of Israel; and he shed innocent blood. Then the Assyrians came and took him prisoner, and carried him in chains to Babylon; but, upon his repentance, he was restored to his throne, and led a humble and pious life for many years, and was buried at last in the garden of his own house at Uzza.

His son, Amon, however, was a wicked man, and did evil for two years, and then his servants killed him. The crown now came to Amon's son, Josiah, who was one of the good children of the Bible. He put down all places of idolatrous worship, and caused the book of God's laws to be publicly read and explained to his people by the priests in the temple, which he had restored and repaired; but he died of a wound received in battle with the Egyptians, and was succeeded by his son Jehoahaz, who was soon dethroned by the king of Egypt, who placed Eliakim, his brother, on the throne of Judah, and changed his name to Jehoiakim.

CHAPTER VI.

CRIME AND PUNISHMENT.

THIS prince was deaf to the warnings of the prophet Jeremiah, and soon fell into the power of Nebuchadnezzar, king of Babylon, who carried away Daniel and several other princes as captives to Babylon. He, however, permitted Jehoiakim to retain his crown, on condition of his paying large sums of tribute money; and when the king failed to pay this, Nebuchadnezzar deprived him of his crown, put him to death, and made his son Jehoiachin king in his stead—at least, for a short time. But his love of riches soon prevailed, and Nebuchadnezzar came and carried away all the treasures, even the gold and silver vessels out of the temple; and as God had before threatened, the king and the greater number of the Jews were led into captivity in Babylon. Zedekiah, the brother of Jehoiakim, succeeded to the throne, after the departure of his nephew; but he also offended the powerful Nebuchadnezzar, and brought destruction upon himself, his subjects, and his country. Such was the fate of the Jews, or of those two tribes of the Israelites who continued faithful to the descendants of David. They had rebelled against the Lord. Discontented and turbulent, they had despised the rule of the judges He had set over them, and in their obstinacy persisted in having kings who should lead them to battle; and what had been the result? These kings, so greatly desired, had been tyrants, oppressors, and idolaters, and thus the fulfilment of their own wish had brought ruin on the people who forsook God, who had brought them out of Egypt, and given them the land of Canaan for a possession. Let us beware of disobedience.

Now let us see what became of the rest of the Israelites who were offended with Rehoboam, the son of Solomon, and who refused to obey his laws, but revolted and chose for themselves a king named Jeroboam. I told you he was bold and ambitious, and proud of being chosen to govern so many people. He soon built himself a great palace at Shechem, and adorned the city; and then, fearing his subjects would want to go to Jerusalem to worship in the beautiful temple which Solomon had built, he made two large calves of gold, and set them up in different parts of his kingdom; then he called himself the high priest, and taught the people to offer sacrifices to these golden images, which he called their gods. One day, as he was about to offer sacrifices at Bethel, there came a prophet and told him that at some future time there would arise a pious king of Judah, named Josiah, who would destroy this altar. Jeroboam was very angry with this prophet; and as Jeroboam stretched out his hand to seize the prophet, God dried up his arm, so that he could not pull his hand back again; and the altar on which Jeroboam was offering the sacrifices to the golden calf was rent to pieces, and the ashes were thrown off, to prove the truth of the prophet's words. Now, Jeroboam felt that it was of no use to pray to the golden calf to restore his hand, but he entreated the man of God to pray for him to the Lord that his hand might be restored to him, and the prayer was granted. Every word the prophet told to the king came to pass: his people were killed in battle, his cities taken, and he spent his days in guilt and misery, and died unregretted.

CHAPTER VII.

MORE ABOUT THE KINGS.

JEROBOAM was succeeded by his son Nadab, who followed in his evil ways, and, like him, set a bad example to his subjects. But his reign was short, and as he went to lay siege to a city of the Philistines, Baasha, one of his own subjects, smote him to death, and made himself king in his stead. Not content with having killed Nadab, Baasha rested not until he had put every member of the house of Jeroboam to death, which judgment had been foretold by the prophet to Jeroboam's wife. Baasha continued the war which his predecessors had begun against the king of Judah, and he built the city of Ramah, which was in the borders of the kingdom of Judah; but Asa, who, as we have heard, was a good king, conquered several cities by the aid of the king of Syria, and Baasha, finding Asa too strong for him, left off building Ramah. His life and his works were evil. He died, and his son Elah succeeded him. But the crown which had been gained by murder was not long worn in peace by the murderer's son; for, less than two years afterwards, Zimri, one of his captains, found him drinking in the house of his steward, and put him and all his household to death. Zimri then made himself king, but he only enjoyed the throne for a few days. His people conspired against him, and insisted on making Omri their king; and Zimri, being besieged in the city of Tirzah, in despair set fire to his palace, and died in the ruins. There is no peace or comfort for the wicked. Fearfully true is the warning given to us in another part of the Bible, were we are told that mischief shall hunt the violent man.

Omri built himself a new palace at Samaria, and there he made the capital of his country. He was a wicked, selfish king, and taught his people to sin; and his son Ahab was more wicked than any king who had gone before him. Ahab married a handsome but very wicked heathen wife, who persuaded him to build an altar and make a grove for the worship of an idol called Baal. In his reign the prophet Elijah lived. This good man went to Ahab, and announced to him that the Lord would, as a punishment

ELIJAH'S SACRIFICE.

for his wickedness, send a grievous famine upon his country. Many poor people suffered the pains of hunger and thirst for the sin of their ruler, and for following his evil example. On one occasion, he proved to Ahab, by fire that descended from heaven upon a sacrifice, that Baal was no God, and that only the Lord God Almighty was able to hear and answer prayer; and the people, being convinced of their error, put all the priests of Baal to death. Ahab, however, hardened his heart, and only strove to kill the holy prophet; and his pride, obstinacy, and cruelty became greater every day. He, however, proved that he believed in the truth of Elijah's predictions, though he would not reform, by asking the prophet to pray for rain, to save his perishing cattle; and the Lord sent rain at the prophet's prayer.

Ahab, soon after, looked with covetous eyes upon a vineyard belonging to a man of Israel named Naboth, and which joined the king's palace. He wished to purchase this vineyard, or to give another in exchange to Naboth; but Naboth refused to part with his portion. Jezebel, the heathen wife of Ahab, no sooner discovered that her husband was fretting himself ill for envy that he could not obtain Naboth's vineyard, than she wrote false letters, and bribed some wicked men to go and bear false witness against the innocent Naboth, declaring that Naboth had blasphemed God and the king. So Naboth was stoned to death, and the wicked king took possession of the vineyard he had coveted. His wicked action brought him no enjoyment, for God sent a prophet to meet him in the vineyard, and to tell him what dreadful judgments He would send upon him and his family. Ahab was killed in battle some time after, and was succeeded by his son Ahaziah, also an ungodly prince, and a worshipper of idols. Once Ahaziah fell through the lattice of an upper chamber, and hurt himself grievously. He sent messengers to inquire of Baalzebub, the god of Ekron, whether he might recover of his injuries; but Elijah the prophet met them on their way, and desired the messengers to return and tell the king that he should never again come down off his bed. Ahaziah then sent a captain with fifty soldiers, to fetch Elijah; and Elijah, instead of going down, sat upon a hill, and called down fire from heaven; and God sent down fire from heaven, and consumed the captain with his fifty men. Then Ahaziah sent a second captain, with his fifty; and again did Elijah call down fire from heaven, and consumed them. The king sent out a third captain with his fifty soldiers, and, because he cried to Elijah for mercy, Elijah spared their lives, and went down with them to the king, and there he told Ahaziah that he should surely die. After Ahaziah's death, Jehoram, his brother, reigned over Israel. He was not quite so sinful as the rest of the kings of Israel. He made a friendship with Jehoshaphat, king of Judah, who was married to his sister Athaliah, and these two kings subdued the Moabites, who had rebelled. Then came the Syrians to war against Israel, and God permitted Elisha, another of his prophets, to disclose the plans of the Syrians to the king of Israel. And when the king of Syria discovered this, he sent an army to take Elisha prisoner; but Elisha smote them all with blindness, and then led them as captives into the midst of Samaria; and when their eyes were opened, the Syrians found themselves in the presence of the king of Israel. The king asked Elisha what he should do to the men, and Elisha told him to give them food and send them back to their master. Benhadad, however, was not grateful for this generous conduct; he laid siege to Samaria, and shut it up so closely that the poor people were all nearly starved for want of food; they could not get out of their gates to buy any provisions, and so horrible was the famine, that the poor mothers ate their own children to appease their hunger. When the king saw to what misery they were reduced, he threatened to kill Elisha as the cause of it, but Elisha told him that the next day food would be plentiful. That same night the Lord frightened the Syrian army so that they fled, and left behind them all their provisions: and the Israelites went out and plundered the tents, and took the food, and all the garments and valuables the Syrians had left.

In due time, the Lord brought to pass the judgments He had pronounced against the descendants of Ahab. He sent Elisha to a young captain named Jehu, and desired him to anoint him king of Israel; and then Jehu went at once to Jezreel, and he shot Jehoram through the heart, and made himself king. And when Jezebel, the king's mother, looked out at a window, Jehu called out and desired her attendants to throw her down; and they threw her out of the window; and Jehu trampled her under the feet of his horses, so that the dogs devoured her, as the prophet Elijah had foretold. Jehu then destroyed all the children of Ahab, and his grandchildren, and caused all

THE KINGS OF ISRAEL AND JUDAH.

DEATH OF JEZEBEL.

the worshippers of Baal to be put to death. Jehu himself did many wicked acts, and permitted his subjects to worship the golden calves I spoke of before. After his death the crown came to his son Jehoahaz, who, by his sins, incurred the anger of the Lord; and the Syrians oppressed the Israelites, so that they were obliged to dwell in tents. After Jehoahaz, reigned Joash, his son. Although Joash was not a good man, he was a great warrior, and gained three victories over the Syrians, and even conquered Amaziah, king of Judah; and, as we have before read, he spoiled the temple and carried off the treasures. His son, Jeroboam, also followed the evil ways of his forefathers; his people were oppressed by their enemies, but Jeroboam was a brave king, and fought for them, and recovered several towns which the Syrians had taken from the Jews; and when he died there was great confusion, and no king was placed upon the throne for some years. At length Zachariah, the son of Jeroboam, was made king, but was killed after a reign of a few months; and others filled the throne, for a few days or weeks, until the Assyrians overran the whole country, and took Samaria by storm, after a siege of three years, and took Hoshea, the king, prisoner, and shut him up, and carried away most of his subjects as captives, about the same time that the Jews were taken captives to Babylon. You know God had threatened the people that their kings would cause them great sorrow; and yet He for many years bore with their ingratitude and wickedness, and beheld the very people for whom He had wrought such great wonders bowing down to blocks of wood and stone; but when they became too much hardened to understand His mercy, then the Lord suffered their kingdom to be destroyed. Yet, upon their repentance and amendment, His merciful ear was open to their cry. He brought them, a small remnant, back again to their own land, and permitted them to rebuild the beautiful temple, prompted and assisted by their prophets, Ezra and Nehemiah.

Half Hours with the Bible.

THE PROPHETS.

CHAPTER I.

MELCHIZEDEK, BALAAM, AND GIDEON.

FROM the time of Moses, the great leader who brought the Israelites out of Egypt, through all the time of the judges and kings of Israel, it frequently happened that the Lord made use of the mouths of men, whereby to announce his intentions towards the Jews. Thus men were sent from God to proclaim what the Lord would do for the deliverance or for the punishment of his people. Alas! it was generally God's wrath for disobedience and idolatry that these good men had to announce; for the Jews were a hard-hearted and stubborn people. These men were called prophets. They were inspired by God's Spirit to foretell what would happen to others at a time when there was no Bible; and some of these prophets suffered many hardships for their love to God, and for doing his service. From their history we may learn how wonderfully God took care of his servants, and how he preserved the lives of those who obeyed his words.

The first prophet mentioned in Scripture after the flood was Melchizedek, who was a prophet, a priest, and a king. He lived in the time of Abraham, whom he blessed, saying, "Blessed be Abram of the most high God." Moses was a prophet; indeed, he was in some respects the greatest of the prophets. Joshua, his successor, prophesied for the benefit of the people over whom God had appointed him to judge. After the death of Joshua, a prophetess, named Deborah, dwelt under a palm tree; and judged the people of Israel, whom she directed to go out against their enemies, and to win a great battle. One of her songs, giving an account of the battle, and of God's mercy, is written in the Book of Judges. This song sets forth that it was God, and not the ten thousand fighting men of the Israelites, who had gained the victory; for it is God alone who can enable us to conquer. Without his help we are lost.

A very great example and warning is offered to us in the history of a prophet who lived at the time when the Israelites had not yet conquered Canaan. His name was Balaam. His history shows how a man may bring ruin on himself by being greedy and covetous.

Balak, a heathen prince, who lived near the camp of

THE PROPHETS.

BALAAM AND THE ANGEL.

the Israelites, before they reached the land of Canaan, applied to Balaam, and offered him great gifts if he would curse the Lord's people. Balaam would have done so for the sake of gain, had not the Lord refused to let him go with the messengers. But afterwards, when he persisted in going on his wicked errand, God sent an angel to meet him on the way with a drawn sword. The ass on which Balaam rode saw the angel, though Balaam did not; and three times the ass turned aside out of the way to avoid the angel. Balaam struck the ass each time. The third time he did this, God miraculously opened the mouth of this poor dumb beast, who spoke to Balaam, and justified her conduct. Balaam's eyes were opened, and he saw the angel, and said, "I have sinned." Then God suffered Balaam to proceed on his journey, and told him that the words he was to speak should be put into his mouth. So, instead of cursing the Israelites, all his words were words of blessing. He lost the reward that Balak had promised to bestow upon him, and was afterwards killed by the Israelites in their war with the Midianites. Gideon, the son of Joash, was another great prophet. The angel of the Lord found him threshing wheat, and said to him, "Hail, thou mighty man of valour." And Gideon became a great leader of the Israelites, and prophesied unto them.

CHAPTER II.

ABOUT THE PROPHET SAMUEL.

SAMUEL was the next prophet of whom we read in the Bible. At the time of his birth, the word of the Lord seldom came to his people, and no prophet seems to have been able to foretell events for some time, until God called Samuel, when he was but a little child, and told him what evil He would bring upon the

THE PROPHETS. 205

SAMUEL ANOINTING DAVID.

high priest Eli, and his disobedient sons, Hophni and Phinehas. After the death of Eli, Samuel was priest and ruler of the Israelites. He helped them to fight against their enemies, the Philistines, and he judged the Israelites for many years. While they hearkened to his voice and obeyed him, they were safe and happy, because he taught them to love the Lord their God, and to serve him.

The people became self-willed, discontented, and unhappy. They declared they would have a king of their own to rule over them. The good Samuel went to his God for counsel in all his difficulties; so he prayed to God to tell him what to do. God was very angry at the ingratitude of the Israelites; but he granted their request, and told Samuel to anoint Saul, who was a very tall, fine young man, to be king over the people; and, instead of being jealous or angry, Samuel tried very hard to teach Saul to do his duty as a king. After he had anointed Saul to be king over Israel, he taught the people their duty to their new king, and wrote it down in a book, to help them to remember it.

Although Samuel knew that God would disappoint the people, and make Saul an occasion of much sorrow to his subjects, he called them together again not long before his death, and talked to them very kindly and very solemnly. He reminded them how they had dwelt in safety without a king, and yet had not been content, but had insisted upon having one. And now he said, " Behold the king whom ye have chosen, and whom ye have desired. If ye will fear the Lord and serve him, and obey his voice, and not rebel against the commandment of the Lord, then shall ye also, and the king that reigneth over you, continue following the Lord your God. But if ye will not obey, then shall the hand of the Lord be against you, as it was against your fathers." And to prove that the words he spoke were put into his heart by God, Samuel called unto the Lord, and the Lord sent a storm of thunder and rain, and the people feared greatly, and acknowledged their sin. Then Samuel comforted them very kindly, promising that if they would follow after God, all would be well. He continued—"The Lord will not forsake his people, for his great name's sake; for it hath pleased the Lord to make you his people. Only fear the Lord, and serve him in truth with all your heart; for consider what great things he hath done for you. But if ye shall still do wicked things, ye shall be consumed, both ye and your king."

Then Samuel went home; and he judged the people no more. But he lived long enough to see Saul proud and self-willed, bringing trouble on himself and his people, and going on from one disobedience to another, until he took upon himself to offer sacrifices to God, instead of waiting for Samuel, who alone, as a priest and a prophet, ought to have done this. Then God sent Samuel to tell Saul that he was so much displeased at his pride and impatience, that he would presently take away his kingdom, and give it to a better man than he. Samuel obeyed God, though he was very sorry in his heart for Saul, whom he had loved very much ever since he had anointed him king. But the Lord told him not to mourn for Saul any longer, but to go and find a young shepherd lad named David, whom he should anoint as king over Israel in the stead of Saul. And Samuel obeyed the Lord, and went and anointed David to be king; but David did not really reign over the people until after the death of Saul. And Samuel returned and dwelt at Ramah, where he died, being old and full of years; and the Israelites mourned for Samuel many days. He had spent his long life in loving and serving God, and now his soul was taken to heaven to be happy with his Maker in glory.

CHAPTER III.

NATHAN AND OTHER PROPHETS.

NATHAN was a prophet who was sent to reproach king David when he fell into sin, and he also counselled and instructed him how to build a house for the Lord. But that same night, after he had spoken to David, the word of the Lord came to Nathan, and told him that David should not build the house which he wished to build, but that his son should be a man of peace, and he should build a beautiful temple. And Nathan came and told David all that God had said. Some years after this, Nathan was appointed by God to anoint Solomon, the son of David, to be king in the room of his father; and we are told in the Bible how Zadok the priest, and Nathan the prophet, anointed Solomon king; and all the people cried, "God save king Solomon!"

THE PROPHETS. 209

NATHAN THE PROPHET.

One prophet there is whose name we do not know. He is mentioned in the Bible only as "the disobedient prophet;" and the history of his fate may be read with advantage by us all. God had given him the gift of prophecy. He who had been endowed with that wonderful power, so that he could tell what would happen, knew what was right; but, alas! he did that which was sinful, and God punished him for his sins. Rehoboam, the son of Solomon, who was anointed king after his father's death, displeased the people, so some of them rebelled against him, and chose another man, named Jeroboam, to be king over them. This Jeroboam, who was styled the king of Israel, was a very wicked man. He not only followed false gods himself, but he persuaded the people that they need not go up to the holy temple at Jerusalem, where Rehoboam the king of Judah, dwelt, but that they would do better to worship two golden calves that he had set up in Bethel and in Dan. One day, when he was burning incense upon one of these altars, God sent a prophet to warn him what would happen hereafter. And when the prophet spoke to the altar, behold, it was rent, and the ashes were poured out upon the ground. Then Jeroboam, in great anger, put out his hand to seize hold of the prophet; but, behold, the hand of the king was withered up in an instant, so that he had no more power to move it again. Jeroboam was greatly alarmed, and very penitent for his sin; and he said unto the man of God, "Intreat for me that my hand may be restored me again."

Wicked as he was, Jeroboam believed that God's prophet was able to do whatever God permitted; and he felt that his own prayers would be of no avail, because he had followed after idols, and had not worshipped the one true God, and trusted in him. So the prophet besought the Lord, and the hand of Jeroboam was restored to him again. Then Jeroboam offered the man of God a reward, and wished him to go into his house and refresh himself; but the prophet answered, "If thou wilt give me half thine house, I will not go in with thee, neither will I eat bread nor drink water in this place. For so it was charged me by the word of the Lord, saying, Eat no bread nor drink water, nor return again by the way thou camest." So he returned home by a different road, and thus far all

THE MEETING OF THE TWO PROPHETS.

was well. The prophet had performed his errand, and had discharged his office faithfully. But now he grew careless, so that, in the time of temptation, he was not watching, and he fell.

There met him by the way an old prophet. This old

prophet had heard of the wonderful things that had been done in Bethel; and he followed after the man of God and persuaded him to return with him, saying, "Come home and eat bread with me." And when the man of God refused, the old prophet again tempted him, by telling him that an angel had appeared unto him, and told him to bring the man of God back to his house, and there to provide him with bread and water. Now this was quite false, and the man of God should have hearkened to the words of the Lord, and to none other; but he persuaded himself that the words of the old prophet were true, because he wished to believe them; and he went and ate with him. While they sat at table, there came a message from God, saying that the man who had disobeyed the Lord should not be buried in the sepulchre of his fathers.

And it came to pass that, as he rode homewards upon an ass, a lion came forth and slew him; but the lion did not devour the dead body, nor did he kill the ass. The lion was found standing by the side of the body, to the surprise of all who heard it. This was the punishment of disobedience. And when the old prophet, who had deceived the man of God and lured him from his duty, heard what had happened, he mourned over him, and went after the body, and buried it in his own sepulchre. But his sorrow could not undo the mischief that had been done, nor could his tears restore life to the disobedient prophet.

THE PROPHETS.   213

CHAPTER IV.

MORE GREAT PROPHETS.

MIRACLES and messages had no effect upon Jeroboam; he still continued very wicked. Then God sent sickness and sorrow into his house. His little son was very ill indeed: and, in his trouble, Jeroboam remembered another prophet, named Ahijah, who had foretold his being made king many years before, and who was now a very old man. So he sent his wife with a present, to ask the prophet God's will concerning the child; and, although she disguised herself, because she did not wish to be known, Ahijah, to whom God had made his will known, heard her as soon as she reached the door, and cried out, "Come in, thou wife of Jeroboam; I know thee, and I have a fearful message unto thee from the Lord. God will punish Jeroboam, whom He hath made king over ten tribes; He will send evil upon thy house, and on thy family; the dogs shall eat their flesh in the city, and the birds shall eat their dead bodies in the field. But the child who is sick shall die in peace, and be buried and mourned, because he loves God; and God in mercy will take him to heaven, and from the trouble to come. Go home, and when thou comest thither, the child shall die." And so it was, that as the mother's feet entered the door of the house, the Lord took away the soul of the child, and he was dead. This was another instance of God's showing His prophets what would be done in time to come.

Some time after the death of Jeroboam, God raised up a very holy prophet, one of the greatest and wisest among all who were sent to the Jews. His name was Elijah. He lived in the days of Ahab, a very wicked king, who worshipped idols, and one idol in particular, called Baal; and on account of this idolatry, God sent many troubles upon Ahab and his people. One of these trials was a sore famine. To show the people that it was not by chance that this sore calamity came upon them, God sent his prophet Elijah to tell Ahab that there should be neither dew nor rain upon the land for a long time, and that, in consequence of this, there would be neither corn, nor fruits, nor grass, nor even a drop of water to drink. All this came to pass; but, for fear Ahab should put him to death as the cause of this famine, Elijah was obliged to hide himself among the rocks. God, however, took care of him; for near his hiding-place was a little brook, called Cherith, and for a long time the brook was well supplied with water, and ravens came every morning and every evening, and brought him bread and flesh to eat. After a time, however, the brook was quite dried up; but God did not suffer his servant to thirst, for the word of the

Lord came to Elijah, saying, " Arise, get thee to Zarephath, which belongeth to Zidon, and dwell there; behold, I have commanded a widow woman there to sustain thee." So Elijah obeyed the voice of the Lord. And when he came to the gate of Zarephath, he saw a poor woman gathering sticks. He called to her, and said, " Fetch me, I pray thee, a little water in a vessel, that I may drink;" and as she was going to fetch it, he called to her and said, " Bring me, I pray thee, a morsel of bread in thine hand." And she said, "As the Lord thy God liveth, I have not a cake, but only a handful of meal in a barrel and a little oil in a cruse;" and she went on to say that she was gathering a few sticks to bake a cake of this for herself and her son, and when that was done they must die of hunger. But Elijah told her not to fear, for that the barrel of meal should not waste, nor should the cruse of oil fail, until the Lord should send rain upon the earth. And it was as he had said. Upon this meal and this oil they were all supported many days. God, however, thought fit to try the poor woman's faith, and to show her the wonderful power of his prophet, by taking the life of her child. While Elijah abode in the house with her, her child died. She thought God had done this to punish her for her sins, and she ran to tell the prophet of her woe; so he took the poor dead child out of his mother's arms, and carried him up to his own room, and there he prayed earnestly to God that the child might live again. And the Lord

ELIJAH RAISETH THE WIDOW'S SON.

heard the prayer of Elijah, and the soul of the child came into him again, and he revived. And Elijah brought down the child alive, gave him to his mother, and said to her, "See, thy son liveth!" And the woman said to Elijah, "Now by this I know that thou art a man of God, and that the word of the Lord in thy mouth is truth."

CHAPTER V.

ELIJAH AND AHAB.

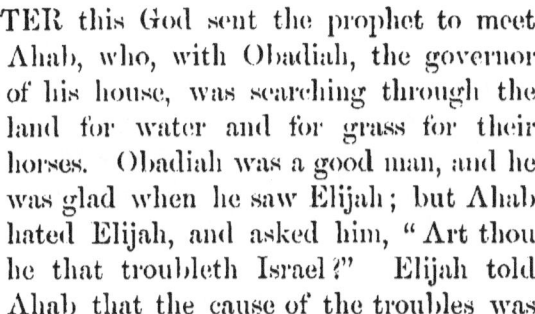
AFTER this God sent the prophet to meet Ahab, who, with Obadiah, the governor of his house, was searching through the land for water and for grass for their horses. Obadiah was a good man, and he was glad when he saw Elijah; but Ahab hated Elijah, and asked him, "Art thou he that troubleth Israel?" Elijah told Ahab that the cause of the troubles was because Ahab and his people were worshippers of Baal; "and now come with the priests of Baal to Mount Carmel," he said, "and let us see who is the true God." So Ahab and all his wicked prophets, four hundred and fifty of them, came to meet Elijah, and many of the people of Israel were there also. Then Elijah said to them all, "Choose now this day whom ye will serve. If Baal be the true God, serve Baal; but if God be the Lord, then follow him." And he commanded the priests of Baal to build an altar, and to put wood upon it; to put no fire under, but to call upon Baal to answer them by sending fire, if he were really God. But they waited, and prayed, and called upon Baal in vain, for there was no fire come

upon the sacrifice. Then they became desperate, and cut themselves with knives and lancets till the blood gushed out upon them. Baal, who was only an idol of wood or stone, could neither hear nor answer them. Then Elijah built up an altar and laid a bullock upon it, and poured water upon it; and then he prayed to his God, the Lord God of Israel. And the Lord heard the prayer of Elijah, and he sent fire from heaven and consumed the sacrifice and the wood, and dried up the water; and the people who saw it cried aloud, "The Lord, he is God! the Lord, he is God!" Then Elijah commanded those who really believed in God to put all the followers of Baal to death, and they did so; but Ahab and his people were spared. And not long after this, God sent rain upon the earth in answer to the seven times repeated prayer of his holy prophet. There came a little cloud out of the sea like a man's hand, and it spread over all the sky, and the rain gushed plentifully down. But, although all the people were thankful, Jezebel, the wicked wife of Ahab, sought to kill Elijah. After having been fed by an angel, and afterwards enabled to fast forty days, Elijah was sent to anoint Hazael to be king of Syria, and Jehu to be king of Israel; and Elisha, a good man, who was ploughing in the field, to be his servant, that he might learn to prophesy after Elijah should have gone.

Very peaceful and glorious was the departure of the good and righteous Elijah. When God had no longer

THE PROPHETS.

any work for him to do, He suffered him to go to Bethel, accompanied by Elisha, the servant whom he had chosen, and he told him that he was going away to heaven, but that after he was gone Elisha would have to do God's messages in his place. And all the prophets knew that God was going to take Elijah from the earth: but Elisha could not bear to speak or to hear about losing his dear master, but he watched and listened to all Elijah said and did; and he saw him smite the waters of the river Jordan with his mantle, and the waters divided, so that Elisha and his master walked over on dry ground. And when Elijah asked him what he should give him, or what he should do for him before they parted, Elisha answered, "Let a double portion of thy spirit be upon me." But Elijah could not give the Holy Spirit to his servant. No; he could only pray to God to bestow his grace upon him. And while he was talking to him, and giving Elisha good advice, there appeared beside them horses of fire, and a chariot of fire; and Elijah was taken away from Elisha, and carried up into heaven in a whirlwind; And Elisha could only cry after him, saying, "My father, my father; the chariot of Israel and the horsemen thereof!" When Elisha could no longer see his master, he rent his clothes, and gathered up the mantle that had fallen from Elijah, and he carried it in great anxiety to the bank of the river. He longed to know whether his prayer had been granted; and he smote the waters of

ELISHA IN THE FIERY CHARIOT.

Jordan with the mantle, as Elijah had done; and, behold, the waters fled back as they had done before, and Elisha crossed on dry land. He felt that God had granted the prayers of Elijah, and he knew that His Spirit would enable him to work miracles: and the other prophets saw it, and said, "The spirit of Elijah doth rest upon Elisha," and they treated him with great respect. And Elisha was enabled, by God's Spirit, to work many miracles for the sons of the prophets. While he was at Jericho, the people were grieving because their land was barren, and

THE PROPHETS.

the waters were bitter; so, when Elisha heard their complaints, he said, "Bring me a cruse of salt;" and he went to the spring of the waters and threw in the salt, and said, "Thus saith the Lord, I have healed these waters. There shall be no more dry and barren land." And this was found to be true; the people now had fertile land and good, pure water. And, as God gave him power to help the needy, so he had also the means of punishing the wicked. Some wicked children followed him, jeering and mocking at him, and crying, "Go up, thou bald-head!" Then Elisha cursed them in the name of the Lord; and there came two she-bears out of the wood, and tore forty-two of them to pieces.

The poor widow of one of the prophets came to Elisha in great distress, because her husband had died in debt. The person to whom the money was due, finding that the widow had nothing wherewith to pay him, had threatened to sell both her sons for slaves. Elisha pitied this poor woman; he said, "What hast thou in the house?" She replied that she had only a pot of oil. Elisha told her to borrow of her neighbours a great many empty vessels; and when she had obtained them, he told her to go home, and shut the door, and to fill as many of these vessels as she could from the pot of oil; and when she had filled them, there was still as much oil left in the pot as before. God multiplied it, as he had done the meal of the poor widow at Zarephath. When all the vessels

THE WIDOW'S OIL MULTIPLIED.

were filled, Elisha told the widow to sell the oil, and first to pay her debts, and then there would be still money to supply the wants of the family. Elisha was always glad to show kindness to the poor and humble, and he was grateful to those who were kind to him. A good woman at Shunem always kept a room ready for him, and was pleased when he went to her house. She had no child, and Elisha, wishing to show his gratitude to her, asked God to give her a son. She was very happy, and thanked God and Elisha for this dear child. One day the child

THE PROPHETS.

went out in the field with his father, and he was ill, and cried to his father, "My head, my head!" and he sat on his mother's knees till noon, and then died. When the poor mother saw that her child was dead, she carried him up, and laid him on Elisha's bed; and then she went to find the prophet and tell him her grief. As soon as the good man knew what had happened, he sent his servant, Gehazi, to go before and lay his staff upon the child's face; but the child was stiff and cold. Elisha followed with the poor mother, and he went in, and prayed to God to restore the child to life. He was not able of himself to raise the dead, but God heard his prayers, and the breath came back into the body of the dead child; and he called the woman, and said, "Take up thy son." Her child was alive and well, and she bowed herself to the ground in thankfulness, and took up her child, and went out. At another time he found the sons of the prophets almost starving with hunger, for there was a famine in the land. He advised them to make some pottage, or vegetable soup, into which, by accident, one of the men put some poisonous herb, and when they came to eat it together, they cried out, "There is death in the pot!" Hungry as they were, they knew that the poison would kill them; so they dared not eat of it until Elisha cast some meal into it, which made it good and wholesome. God it was, and not the meal, who removed the poison; but on this account did Elisha receive the more honour from those who beheld the miracle. He had a kind friend, who provided him with food during the famine; but Elisha would not keep all for himself, and he fed an hundred men with a few loaves, and when they had satisfied their hunger, some was left for another day. One of his greatest deeds was when he cured the leprosy of Naaman, a rich captain from the land of Syria; but he would take no reward for this, and because Gehazi, his servant, told a lie to induce Naaman to give him money and garments, he was made the instrument of punishing this Gehazi, who was covetous, false, and deceitful. Although Elisha knew God would punish him in another world if he did not repent, yet he brought a dreadful punishment upon him: Gehazi was smitten with leprosy, that he might prove an example to others.

In time, the prophets, who were very numerous, came and asked Elisha to let them build a dwelling-place on the banks of the Jordan; and, while they were cutting down wood, the axe, which was made of iron, slipped, and fell into the river. The man was very sorry, and ran to Elisha, saying, "Alas, master!" for it was borrowed, and he was too poor to buy another. Elisha was always ready to help the poor and unfortunate. He had no money to give him, but he cut down a stick, and threw it into the water just where the heavy iron had sunk down, and the axe head rose directly to the top, and swam on the water. Then Elisha said, "Take it up;"

THE PROPHETS.

and the poor man went thankfully to his work again. God's power, at Elisha's word, made a heavy piece of iron to swim; and the people, who saw the miracles which Elisha performed, respected him, and feared God. And soon after this the king of Syria, having discovered that Elisha was able to reveal all his doings and his movements to Joram, the king of Israel, whom he was trying to conquer, sent, therefore, his soldiers by night to take Elisha prisoner. The servant of this good man was frightened when he saw the city surrounded with soldiers and horses; but Elisha, who trusted in God, was not afraid. He first opened the eyes of his servant to behold the chariots and horses of fire which God had placed around to protect them, and he afterwards struck the whole army of the Syrians with blindness, and in this state he led them into the heart of the city, and there he prayed to God to open their eyes again. You may believe the Syrians were much alarmed when they found themselves surrounded by their enemies; but, instead of having them put to death, he advised the king to give them meat and drink, and let them go home to tell the wonderful story. But, when the famine grew sore in the land, the foolish king of Israel began to fancy that Elisha was the cause of the famine, for the enemies were all round the city, headed by their king. So he came and threatened to put Elisha to death, but Elisha had no fear: he only told the king and his followers that food should be plentiful "by

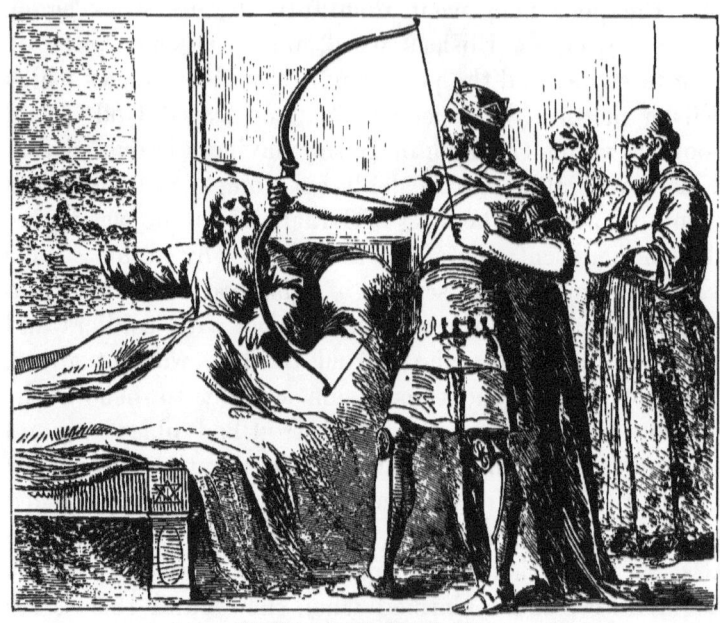

ELISHA ON HIS DEATH BED.

this time to-morrow." One nobleman would not believe this, and the next day, when the words of Elisha came true, he was trodden to death in the crowd. After performing many other miracles, and serving God very faithfully for many more years, he fell ill and died, and was buried; but even after his death God made manifest the wonderful powers with which he had invested this good man; for, long after, as the Israelites were burying a man, they were surprised by some robbers. They threw the body of the dead in their fright into the tomb of Elisha, and ran away; but no sooner did the dead body fall upon the bones of Elisha, than the man was restored to life, so that even the bones of Elisha were honoured and esteemed.

Some time after Elisha's death, the Ten Tribes of Israel were carried into captivity, and during the years of captivity God raised up to them two prophets, named Ezra and Nehemiah. They assisted the Jews to rebuild the "Temple," after their return to their own land. Each of them wrote a book, which is called after the name of the prophet, and although they did not live before others that are afterwards mentioned, they are first placed in the Bible, and therefore I mention them here also.

CHAPTER VI.

THE REMAINING PROPHETS.

THE story of Jonah is full of interest. He was not so good a man as Elisha, but he was sent by God to preach to the people of Nineveh, and to tell them what punishment God would bring upon them if they continued in sin; but Jonah was disobedient, and got into a ship, and tried to sail away into another country. Then God sent a frightful storm, and Jonah was cast into the sea, and swallowed by a large fish, which God had prepared to swallow him; and for three days and nights God kept him alive in the belly of the whale, until God ordered the fish to cast Jonah up on the dry land again. Jonah was humbled by this punishment, and grateful for his deliverance, so he made haste to go to Nineveh and fulfil the Lord's commands.

After him arose a good prophet, named Isaiah, who wrote a great many chapters in the Bible, and foretold the birth and sufferings of the Messiah; and he was sent with messages to Hezekiah, the king of Judah, and with words of warning to the people of Israel and Judah.

The next book was written by a prophet called Jeremiah, who was descended from Aaron. He prophesied for several years, principally foretelling the miseries God would bring upon the Jews.

THE PROPHETS. 229

JONAH WAS CAST INTO THE SEA.

Ezekiel foretold the ruin of the Jews and of their enemies, and promised that after their captivity God would visit his people.

Daniel, a young Jewish prince, and a captive, was called to interpret a very wonderful dream, which had troubled the mind of King Nebuchadnezzar, and which none of the king's astrologer's or magicians were able to comprehend. But God revealed the meaning to Daniel during the night, and when he had interpreted the dream the king fell upon his face and worshipped Daniel and his

God; and he gave him gifts, and made him ruler of the whole province. Daniel afterwards interpreted to Belshazzar, the son of Nebuchadnezzar, the meaning of some words that were traced upon the wall by a part of a hand during a feast given by the king, and that night the kingdom was taken by Darius, the Mede, and Belshazzar was slain, even as Daniel had foretold. Darius, the conqueror, having heard of the wonderful talents of Daniel, made him a chief ruler among the people, and had intended to put the whole kingdom under him. This made others jealous and envious; but because they could find no fault in Daniel, nor aught to accuse him of, they persuaded the king that no person should ask anything for thirty days, save of the king himself; and the king listened to their foolish counsel, and made a decree that whosoever should break the law should be cast into the den of lions.

The fear of this dreadful death did not deter Daniel from praying three times a day. So the envious princes told the king that Daniel "regarded neither the king nor the decree which he had signed," and that he must be put to death. In vain did the king regret the folly he had been guilty of, and strive all day to find some means of saving Daniel; for his word's sake, he was obliged to have him cast into the den of lions, which was covered with a stone, and sealed with the king's seal. God, however, shut the mouths of the lions, so that Daniel took no harm; and Darius the king was overjoyed to find him

THE PROPHETS.

DANIEL CAST INTO THE DEN OF LIONS.

alive in the morning. And he made a decree that all the people of the kindom should fear and tremble before the God of Daniel, for that there was no other God, who could deliver after this manner. So Daniel lived in honour, and prophesied many years; and the book in which these things are written is called by his name.

The books of Hosea and Joel follow. Many and sad are the denunciations against Egypt and the enemies of the Lord's people.

Amos also denounces vengeance upon the enemies of the

Jews; he warns his fellow-countrymen of their sins, of idolatry, their ingratitude, and their contempt of the Sabbath.

Obadiah wrote one short prophecy, predicting Christ's kingdom.

Micah strove hard to convince the Jews of their sin and danger, and bring them to repentance. His book also foretells the coming and the mercy of Christ.

Nahum writes principally about the fall of Nineveh.

Habakkuk mourns over the wickedness of the Jews, and concludes his book with a beautiful prayer to God, in whom he rejoices.

Zephaniah foretold the desolation of Judah and Jerusalem, and predicted the future glory of the Jewish nation.

Haggai is supposed to have flourished during the captivity of the Jews in Babylon; but his prophecies were not made public until sixteen years after their return to Canaan when he encouraged them in rebuilding their Temple.

Zechariah was a prophet who aided Haggai in his efforts to direct the Jews, and to bring them to repentance. He mentions nine different visions which had been revealed to him by God; and preaches to them of deliverance, and of the triumphs of the Gospel.

Malachi, though last mentioned in the Bible, is not positively the last prophet who prophesied to the Jews. He forbade, in God's name, their heathen marriages and other things which were displeasing to God, and warned them of the coming of OUR LORD JESUS CHRIST.

Half Hours with the Bible.

THE GOOD CHILDREN OF SCRIPTURE.

CHAPTER I.

THE CHILDREN ISHMAEL AND ISAAC.

 I AM going to tell you some short stories about the good children that are mentioned in the Bible, that you may hear what happened to them; and then you may all try to follow their good examples. Solomon, who was a very wise king, has written, "Even a child is known by his doings, whether his work be pure, and whether it be right."

The heart of a child is like a garden in spring-time, all ready to bring forth flowers and fruit, according to the seed that is planted therein. The good seed is the instruction that is given by kind parents and teachers; but if this good seed do not sink into the heart, there grow up evil weeds

—pride, obstinacy, and deceit. Now, just as the gardener watches for these weeds, to pull them up so soon as they appear, so should every child watch and pray to be delivered from sin, and try to pluck out each bad feeling from its heart. Then be grateful, dear children, to those who teach you, and help you to store your minds in early youth; because where good lessons are unlearned, there is the more room left for evil thoughts and bad feelings to grow.

The best store of knowledge that can make even a little child wise and good is to be found in the Holy Scriptures; and our Lord Jesus Christ said to those who came to hear him, "Search the Scriptures; for in them ye think ye have everlasting life; and those are they which testify of me."

Ishmael is the first *child* mentioned in the Bible; he was a son of Abraham and of a bondwoman named Hagar, who lived with Sarah, Abraham's wife. Ishmael was a quick, clever boy, and was very kindly treated by Abraham; but it came to pass that God gave Sarah a son, according to His promise. Ishmael was at that time old enough to know right from wrong, and to refrain from giving offence by his conduct; but he behaved very rudely, and roughly mocked at his little brother, and also at Sarah; so that to appease Sarah, who was very angry, Abraham was obliged to send him away with Hagar his mother. They would both have perished of thirst and heat in the wilderness, had not God in His mercy sent an angel to Hagar to show her a well of water; and the angel comforted her, and told her that God would make Ishmael the head of a great nation. So the child was spared, and he lived to be a great and rich prince among the Arabs.

Meanwhile Isaac, who was called the child of promise, and with reason, for he had been promised by God to Abraham and Sarah, and was also to inherit the promises made by God to Abraham, grew up. He was good and gentle, and obedient to his parents in all things. When he was grown a great lad, God wished to try the faith of both Abraham and Isaac. He knew the hearts of both, but still he made a trial of the love of the one, and of the obedience of the other. To prove that Abraham really loved his God more than he loved his only child, God ordered the kind father to take his son and offer him up, as lambs and other animals used to be offered on an altar, as a sacrifice to Him. Abraham saddled his ass, cut down wood for burnt offering, and went to the land of Moriah, where God had told him to offer this terrible sacrifice. When they came to the place, Isaac carried the wood, upon which his father intended to sacrifice him; and he suffered himself to be bound, and laid upon the altar; and Abraham stretched forth his hand, armed with a knife, to slay his son, whom he loved, because God had commanded it. But when God had thus proved his faithful servants, He stayed the hand of Abraham, just as he had raised the knife to slay his darling son; and God, by the mouth of an angel, showed him a ram that was caught by the horns, in a thicket close by; and the Lord told Abraham to offer up this ram as a sacrifice instead of his son.

And God made a promise to Abraham, saying, "Because thou hast not withheld from me thy son, thine only son; in blessing I will bless thee, and in multiplying I will multiply thy seed (or family) as the stars of heaven, and as the sand which is upon the sea shore, because thou hast obeyed my voice."

CHAPTER II.

THE CHILDHOOD OF JOSEPH.

JOSEPH, the grandson of Isaac, was the eldest son of Rachel his mother, who died when he was young; wherefore, he became the favorite child of the patriarch Jacob, his father; who loved him so very dearly, that he indulged him more than all the rest of his children; and he gave him a pretty coat of many colors. This roused the jealousy and ill-will of Joseph's brothers. Each new proof of their father's affection to Joseph made them hate him the more bitterly.

However, the good little Joseph dreamed two very wonderful dreams, which he related to his brethren; they were indeed dreams sent by God, to prepare the mind of Joseph for the changes that would occur. His dreams foreshadowed that his father and brethren would one day bow down before him. His brethren, and even his father rebuked him, for supposing that any such things as he foretold were likely to occur. But the envy of his brethren was now so great that they determined to kill the poor boy. So one day, when he went out to them in the field where they were keeping their flocks at some distance from home, they wished to put him to death. One of the brethren, named Reuben, tried to save him, and advised them to cast him into a deep pit. Reuben intended to take Joseph out when they went away, and to take him back to his father. As for the others, they would have left him in the pit to starve, or be devoured by wild beasts. But while they were sitting together eating and drinking, there came by a company of Midianites. To these men they sold their brother Joseph as a slave for twenty pieces of silver; then they killed a kid, and dipped his pretty coat into the blood, to make it appear that the boy had been killed by some wild beast. They brought the coat to Jacob their father, and said, "This have we found; see whether it be thy son's coat or no." And the poor father knew the coat. He said, "It is my son's coat; an evil beast hath devoured him; Joseph is without doubt rent in pieces." And he refused to be comforted, and wept bitterly for his son. What lesson must we learn from this story? To be meek and quiet, forgiving and submissive; for we never find that Joseph, either in word or in deed, returned the ill-will of his unkind brothers.

CHAPTER III.

THE CHILD SAMUEL.

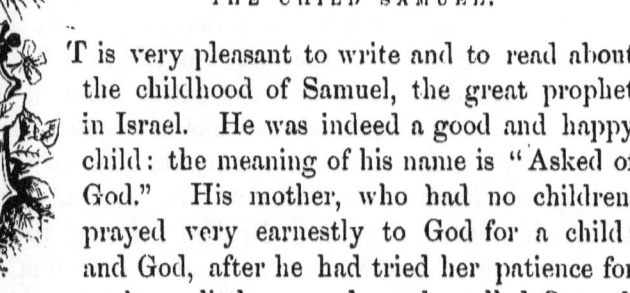

'T is very pleasant to write and to read about the childhood of Samuel, the great prophet in Israel. He was indeed a good and happy child: the meaning of his name is "Asked of God." His mother, who had no children, prayed very earnestly to God for a child; and God, after he had tried her patience for some time, gave her a little son, whom she called Samuel. Hannah sang a psalm to God in her joy; she was so thankful to her Heavenly Father for this child, that she resolved to make the boy God's servant as soon as he could speak. When he was only four years old, she brought him to Eli, the high priest, at Shiloh. The Jews had different forms of religion from ours; that is, they worshipped God in a different manner; and the high priest was at the head of their religious ceremonies, and taught the people what they must do. Therefore, he lived almost always in the house of God: and Hannah wished this good man to teach her little son how to serve the Lord Jehovah. So she placed him under Eli's care, to be taught; but every year she came up to see her beloved child; for she lived a long way off from Shiloh; and she used to bring him a present of a little dress, made of linen. This dress was similar to those worn

SAMUEL AND ELI.

by the priests. It had long sleeves, and came down to his feet, and was called an "ephod." And so Samuel dwelt with Eli; he was a happy child as he ministered or waited upon Eli, and upon the Lord, whose eyes are ever open, beholding the evil and the good; but while the Lord was pleased to behold the seeds of good that were daily expanding in the boy's young heart, He beheld with grief and displeasure the bad conduct and wickedness of the two sons of Eli. This old man loved his God, and in many ways served Him truly; but he over indulged his own children. When they did evil in their childhood, their father was too fond of them to correct or punish them as he ought to have done; and as they grew older, they grew more and more wicked, and disobeyed the commands of God and their kind parent: they cared for nothing but good eating and drinking, and their own pleasures and amusements; and thus they went on from bad to worse, while their father said, "My sons, why do ye so? for I hear of your evil dealings by all this people. Nay, my sons; for it is no good report that I hear: ye make the Lord's people to transgress." By this he meant that the bad example of the high priest's sons led other people to do evil. But these wicked men paid no heed to the words of their father, and they went on still more wickedly; neither did a dreadful message which God sent to their father affect them at all. This was, that he should cause both of these sons to be killed in one day, and that none of Eli's family should be priests after him, because he had not controlled his children better.

Yet for all this they went on in their sins; until one night, when Samuel was sleeping in his little bed some distance from Eli, he heard a voice calling, "Samuel!" Samuel thought that Eli, who was now very old, and whose eyes were so dim that he could hardly see to wait upon himself, wanted him; so he answered quickly, "Here am I;" and he jumped up and ran to Eli to know what he wanted.

Eli, however, answered him, and said, "I called not, lie down again:" and the kind little boy obeyed Eli, and went and lay down. And the Lord called yet again, "Samuel!" and Samuel arose, and went to Eli, and said, "Here am I; for thou didst call me." And Eli answered, "I called not, my son; lie down again." Now Samuel did not yet know the Lord, neither was the word of the Lord revealed unto him. And the Lord called Samuel again the third time; and he arose and went to Eli, and said, "Here am I; for thou didst call me." And now Eli understood that the Lord himself must have called the child; so he said unto him, "Go, lie down; and it shall be if *He* call thee again, that thou shalt say, Speak, Lord: for thy servant heareth:" so Samuel went and lay down in his place.

When God called again, "Samuel, Samuel," then Samuel answered, "Speak; for thy servant heareth." And very sorrowful were the words which the Lord spake unto the child; for He told him of all the evil and punishment that He was going to bring upon Eli and his house, because the weak old man had not restrained his sons from sinning against Him. And the boy dreaded the task of telling Eli the sad truths that God had told him. He did not go near the old man, but went about his business, and began to open the doors round about the tabernacle. This was a part of his duty. However, when Eli called Samuel, the child obeyed at once, and, in answer to the questions of Eli, told him truly all the words that God had said unto him. And Eli, although he was a foolish, weak father, was resigned and submissive to the decrees and commands of God, however grieved he might have felt for all the sorrow that was threatened. He very meekly and properly replied, "It is the Lord: let him do what seemeth him good." Yes, Eli loved God, though he had done wrong, and he now knew that Samuel was a "prophet"—that is, a person to whom God shows the things that are to happen at a future time. And then God permitted the Philistines to make war against the Israelites, who told the priests to bring out the ark into the field; for they wished to be very brave, and to fight like men. God was already displeased with His own people, so He suffered them to be conquered. A very, very great number of the Israelites were killed, and among them were Hophni and Phinehas, the sons of Eli, who had charge of the ark, which also fell into the hands of the Philistines; and they carried it away to one of their own towns. Neither Eli nor Samuel went out to see the battle; but the poor, blind old man sat waiting on a high seat by the gate of Shiloh; for he was very anxious to hear tidings of the ark and of his disobedient sons. And when he heard the sounds of crying, and the tumult, he asked the reason. So a man told him, saying, "Israel is fled before the Philistines, and there hath been also a great

THE GOOD CHILDREN OF SCRIPTURE.   243

slaughter among the people, and thy two sons, Hophni and Phinehas, are dead, and the ark of God is taken." As soon as this poor old man ninety years of age and upwards, heard these sad tidings, and that the ark was taken, he fell down

THE DEATH OF ELI.

backwards off his high seat, and his neck was broken in the fall; so he died. Was not this a sad end for a man who had been God's high priest for so many years? How grieved Samuel must have been for the loss of his kind friend! But he strove the more earnestly to please and serve God; and when the people beheld that the prophecies of this young servant of God came true, they honored him, and believed in his prophecies, and he lived many years as a judge and a prophet in Israel. I dare say you have learned the little hymn about this:—

> "When little Samuel woke,
> And heard his Maker's voice,
> At every word He spoke
> How much did he rejoice!
> Oh, blessed, happy child, to find
> The God of Heaven so near and kind!
>
> Like Samuel, let me say,
> Whene'er I read thy word,
> 'Speak, Lord, I would obey
> The voice that I have heard.
> And when I in thy house appear,
> Speak, for thy servant waits to hear.'"

And this should be the prayer of your own lips, my children, that you may learn in your youthful days to hear the voice of God in your hearts, to love Him, and obey Him.

I must now tell you something that happened when Samuel was an old man. God sent him to choose a very young lad, and to anoint him king over Israel. The merciful Lord had granted the prayers of his discontented people, and given them an earthly king, contrary to His own wishes; and then He suffered this king, who was named

THE GOOD CHILDREN OF SCRIPTURE.

Saul, to act wickedly, and to bring many troubles on his subjects. At length Saul became quite depraved, and God determined to put another king in his place.

So God desired Samuel to fill his horn with oil, and go to Jesse the Beth-lehemite, and anoint one of his sons as king. Six sons of Jesse passed before Samuel, and yet he found that none of them were pleasing to the Lord. So he said to Jesse, "Are here all thy children?" Then Jesse answered, "There remaineth yet the youngest, and, behold, he keepeth the sheep." Then Samuel desired Jesse to send for him; and when David came before Samuel, he beheld only a boy, with a lovely color on his cheeks, and a sweet, pleasant smile, and eyes that looked full of love to God and every one. And the Lord said, "Arise, anoint him: for this is he." And Samuel anointed David king. Then Samuel went back to his own house, and David returned to his occupation of keeping his father's sheep. For, although God gave His spirit to the good lad from that day, He did not wish to make him a king while Saul was alive. David had many things to do to win the love and trust of the Israelites before he must be their king. But God had chosen David while he was a mere child, because he knew the lad was humble, and honest, and brave; and David used to love to play sweet psalms and holy songs upon his harp, to tell of God's wonders and mercies, and of his love to Him. The psalms that we read every day in our prayer books:

246 HALF HOURS WITH THE BIBLE.

DAVID WITH HIS SHEEP.

were some of the sweet songs that David used to sing while he was watching his sheep.

How should we strive, when we read these psalms of praise and thanksgiving, to feel like David in our hearts, that we may deserve, through the blood of Jesus, to wear a crown of gold in heaven, which would be far better than to be a king or a queen on earth!

CHAPTER IV.

THE CHILDHOOD OF JOASH.

OME time after David's death, there was a little boy made king, his father Ahaziah having been killed. His grandmother, who was a very wicked woman named Athaliah, endeavored to put all her grandsons to death, in order that she herself might be made queen. One of them, however, quite a baby, was hidden with his nurse for six years in the house of the Lord; but when he was seven years old, the priests brought this little boy, Joash, into the temple; and, having placed guards at every door, they put the crown upon his head, and all the people shouted, "God save the king." When the wicked queen came out to see the cause of rejoicing, she rent her clothes, and tried to escape, but the soldiers went after her, and put her to death.

And Joash, under the care of the good high priest Jehoiada, did that which was right in the sight of the Lord. He caused a chest to be made, with a hole bored in the lid, and placed it outside the gate of the Lord, that every one of the princes and people might put in what they pleased; and thus they collected a great deal of money to pay for the repairs of the temple, and the priests offered burnt offerings in the house of the Lord continually.

The good old priest lived to be an hundred and thirty years old; but after his death, Joash, by degrees, learned to do evil. He listened to the flattery and foolish words of the princes of Judah; and, forgetting all the kindnesses he had received from the good Jehoiada, he suffered Zechariah, the priest's son, to be stoned to death by these idolators, because he reproved them for their sins. How much the Lord must have been displeased with the ingratitude and cruelty of Joash!

CHAPTER V.

MORE BIBLE CHILDREN.

MUST not forget to mention some children who are spoken of among the prophets, because you will see that God at all times punished the wicked, whether young or old, and rewarded the good.

There was a very good man named Elijah, who was sent by God to live with a poor widow and her son during the time of the famine. This poor woman had only a little meal, and a very small quantity of oil; and just as the prophet Elijah came to her, she was going to make a little cake of this, fearing it was the last meal they were ever likely to get, and knowing that they must soon die of hunger; however, she cheerfully obeyed the word of Elijah, when he desired her first to make a little cake for him; and, according to his promise, the barrel of meal and the oil lasted, although she used some every day, until the rain came and the famine was over. But during this time the little boy fell sick and died, and the poor mother grieved sorely. She feared that Elijah had caused the death of the child, as a punishment for the sins she had committed during her life. But Elijah took the child and carried him up into a loft, and laid him on his own bed. And there he prayed earnestly to God, and stretched himself three times upon the child, and cried to God, saying, "Oh, Lord, my God, I pray thee let this child's soul come into him again." And the Lord heard the prayer of Elijah, and the soul of the child came into him again, and he revived. So Elijah carried him down to his mother, and said, "See, thy Son liveth." And the woman said, "Now by this I know that thou art a man of God, and the word of thy mouth is truth." How could the widow help believing in God, or in his kind prophet Elijah, who had, in the first place, kept her and her son from dying of starvation when many poor people went for days without food, or even water, for when there is no rain for a long time the water springs are dried up; and, still more, for having made her child alive again?—You also should learn from this, that God can do all things. He can hear the softest prayer you make to him; and He will, after your death, make you alive again if you love Him truly; not to live again in this world, but to dwell with Him in heaven. No doubt, his good servant Elisha is also there; he lived with Elijah a long time, and saw many wonderful things which he did; and so, after God had taken Elijah to heaven, He sent His Holy Spirit upon this faithful servant, and He permitted Elisha to perform almost the same miracles that Elijah had done before. Elisha also restored a little boy to life whose mother had been kind to him. She had built a nice little room in her house on purpose for Elisha to sleep in whenever he pleased.

How pleasant is was for him, when he returned from traveling about in God's service, to have a nice quiet room, where he could pray and commune with his Maker! Elisha wished very much to show himself grateful to this good woman, and, after thinking of various things to please her, he remembered, or rather his servant did, that perhaps she would like to have a child. So he sent to call her, and promised her a son; she was very pleased, and after the birth of her dear baby she loved Elisha and his God better than ever for having made her so happy: and she liked to see her child grow strong, and run about after his father. One day, when he had become a great boy, he followed his father into the harvest field, to see the men reaping the corn: but the sun was very hot, and the poor child cried out, "My head, my head!" The father sent one of his servants to carry the child home to his mother. He was in great pain; his mother took him on her knees, and nursed him; but, in spite of all her care, he died at twelve o'clock

THE GOOD CHILDREN OF SCRIPTURE.   251

ELISHA RAISING THE WIDOW'S SON.

on the same day. You may believe that she was in great grief for the loss of her only child. But in her trouble, she thought of her kind friend Elisha: she knew that he had prayed to God to give her this child: and perhaps she had heard that Elijah had restored the child of the poor widow. So she laid the body of her darling on Elisha's bed, and she shut the door, and begged her husband would let her have one of the asses to ride upon, that she might go in search of Elisha; and he allowed her to go, and sent one of his servants with her. As soon as Elisha saw her coming so quickly, he fancied something must have happened, and he sent his servant to meet her, and ask if all was well; and though her heart was almost breaking with sorrow, she answered, "It is well," for she knew that all was right that God did. But when she threw herself at his feet, and said, "Did I ask my Lord for a son?" the prophet understood that her child was dead. And he went with the poor mother, and prayed to God, and he stretched himself over the child, and the child sneezed seven times, and then opened his eyes. And then Elisha called the happy mother, and told her "to take up her son." No doubt, the boy was taught by his mother to love Elisha, and to reverence one to whom God showed such favor.

God also gave Elisha power to punish wicked children. He used to travel about from place to place where God sent him. He was no longer a young man, and his hair was thinned by age and toil. So one day, as Elisha was going up to a town where the people worshipped idols, a great many idle, wicked children came out of the city to play, and when they met Elisha they began to laugh at him, and to mock him, saying, "Go up, thou bald head; go up, thou bald head!"

Now God, who will not hold them guiltless who take His name in vain, was very angry with these wicked children, and Elisha was also angry. He turned round, and told them something dreadful would happen to them; and scarcely had he spoken when two bears came rush-

THE GOOD CHILDREN OF SCRIPTURE.

ing out of a wood near by, and tore forty-and-two of them to pieces.

Tears and screams were all in vain; they could not run away from the punishment God had sent upon them, any more than you could run away from sickness or death. How careful you must be not to treat God's name, or any of His holy things, with mockery, for fear God should punish you! Neither should you laugh at the lame or the blind, nor at any one who is sent to teach you holy things.

CHAPTER VI.

THE STORY OF THE LITTLE MAID; AND OF OTHER CHILDREN.

IT is, however, more pleasant to hear of good children and good people than naughty ones, so I shall change the subject, and tell you of a little captive maid, who had been carried away by the Syrians out of the land of Israel; and she was a slave who waited upon Naaman's wife. Naaman was a great, rich, and honorable captain, but he had a bad disorder called leprosy. This little Hebrew girl loved her mistress and her master, but she remembered her God and His prophet Elisha, whom she reverenced and loved in her early home; and she knew that Elisha could perform wonderful cures. She told her mistress, and at last Naaman was persuaded to go to Israel; and there, by God's mercy, he was sent by Elisha to wash in the river Jordan, and his leprosy was cured. See how much good was done by this pious and affectionate little captive girl! Remember that none are too young to be kind and thoughtful.

Josiah was one of the good kings who came to the crown of Judah when he was only eight years old. He seems to have had a pious mother, and good advisers, for the Bible says " he did that which was right in the sight of the Lord," and turned not aside from "His ways," to the right hand, or to the left. As soon as he was old enough to give orders, he had the Temple repaired. He caused the book of God's laws to be read in the hearing of the people, and he destroyed the temple of the idolaters, and kept a most solemn passover; and there was no Jewish king before or after him that turned to the Lord so faithfully as did the youthful Josiah. Should not his example be a precious one to you? It shows you that even a young king may serve God, and make his people and his countrymen better and happier.

God had not sent His dear Son down on earth to die, when these children were on earth, of whom I have been writing. But you know that more than eighteen hundred years ago He did come upon earth in the form of a little helpless baby, and was called Jesus; that He was worshipped by the wise men in the stable at Bethlehem; that He was saved from the vengeance of Herod by the flight of His mother into Egypt by night; that He lived with His

FLIGHT INTO EGYPT.

parents at Nazareth, and was subject, or obedient, to them, growing daily in wisdom and strength, and the grace of God was upon Him. When He was only twelve years old, He was found in the Temple, sitting amidst the most clever men of those times, both listening to their discourse, and asking them questions, so that all that heard him were astonished at His understanding and His answers.

Jesus, however, immediately answered to the call of His mother, and returned with her to a humble home at Nazareth, where He set to all children an example of dutiful conduct and humility. And such are the children that Jesus loves. When He was on earth He showed His love even for the youngest child. He was pleased when their mothers brought their little children to His feet. He took

CHILDHOOD OF JESUS.

them in His arms; He put His hands on them, and blessed them, saying, "Suffer little children to come unto me, and forbid them not; for of such is the kingdom of heaven." And though Jesus now lives in heaven, on His bright throne, He still loves little children. He calls them to come to Him by prayer, and by faith, and by love; and while on earth He condescended to go to the house of the ruler, and restore to life his little daughter. He took her by the hand, and said unto her, "Maid, I say unto thee, arise;" and He restored her to her parents.

MARY AND MARTHA AND JESUS, HERE.

Jesus was kind to the mothers of these children. He loved his own mother Mary, although she was but a poor woman, and He was the Son of God. Mary Magdalene, Mary and Martha, the sisters of Lazarus, and the poor widow, the woman who had faith, and was cured by touching his garment, all loved him. He taught the truth to

258 HALF HOURS WITH THE BIBLE.

DAVID AND ABIGAIL.

the woman of Samaria; to the Syrophenician woman He restored her sick daughter, and to many others He showed mercy. There are also several good women mentioned in the Bible who deserve to be noticed in this book.

One is Abigail, who showed kindness to the good King David, when her husband Nabal refused to supply his followers with bread and water in their need. Abigail no sooner heard what had happened than she hasted to go forth and meet David with corn and wine, and two hundred loaves of bread, with raisins and figs, and other neces-

THE GOOD CHILDREN OF SCRIPTURE.

RUTH AND NAOMI.

saries, and she bowed herself before David, who was just uttering threats against Nabal and his house, and she begged him to accept her offering. So David blessed Abigail for having prevented bloodshed; and, after her husband's death, he sent for Abigail, and married her.

Ruth, too, the dutiful daughter, who refused to leave her widowed mother-in-law, but followed her into a strange land, and worked for and comforted her. God did not suffer her filial duty to go unrewarded, for he caused her to find favor in the eyes of Boaz, a wealthy farmer, in whose fields she went to glean corn for her mother's use; and afterwards she became his wife, and the mother of a son, from whom Jesus descended.

Esther, a beautiful young Jewess, had been born while the Jews were in captivity; but her beauty and modesty so pleased the King Ahasuerus, or Artaxerxes, as he is sometimes called, that he made her his queen. This king had a minister, named Haman, who greatly disliked the Jews, not knowing that the Queen was a Jewess; he persuaded the king that the Jews were going to rebel against him, and advised him to put them all to death. The king gave his consent to this: and when Mordecai, the queen's uncle, heard this, he went to the palace gate in mourning, and when Esther sent to know the cause, he told her that she and all her people were to be put to death by the king's order, unless she could save them; and the good Esther did really risk her life to save them, by entering the king's presence without being sent for. God, however, moved the heart of the king to speak kindly to Esther; and she then invited the king and Haman to a banquet, and when the king bade her ask any request of him, and it should be granted, she begged for her own life, and that the lives of her people might be spared at her request. The king bade her explain her meaning; and when he found what Haman had done, he ordered him to be hanged, with his ten sons, upon a gallows that he had prepared for Mordecai, of whom he was envious, and whom he had, the day before, been

THE GOOD CHILDREN OF SCRIPTURE. 261

HAMAN AND MORDECAI.

obliged to lead through the city, seated upon the king's own horse, and dressed in royal robes, and to cry before him, "Thus shall it be done unto the man whom the king delighteth to honor." Haman's envy was the cause of his death, and the bravery of Queen Esther saved her uncle's life, and all the Jewish captives.

The wife of Job was not a good woman, although she had for a husband the most patient man that ever lived. God suffered the devil to tempt him, and try him with pains, losses, and bereavements; but nothing could shake

JOB HEARING THE EVIL NEWS.

his faith in God. God sent the thunderbolts, and slew his servants. He caused the housetop to fall in and bury all his children, his oxen and servants were carried away by the Sabeans, his sheep were destroyed by fire; but Job still worshipped God; and when a servant came running to tell him of all these disasters, he did not repine, or rebel against God; but he bowed his head, and said meekly: "The Lord gave, and the Lord hath taken away: blessed be the name of the Lord!"

This was the right way to speak, and thus should we

JOB IN HIS MISFORTUNES.

bear sorrow when it pleases God to afflict us. And you may see him in the picture covered with sores, his house in flames, deserted by his friends, ridiculed by his unholy wife—calmly answering, "What, shall we receive good at the hand of God, and shall we not receive evil?" What a lesson of patience and gratitude to God is taught us by Job! But, in the midst of his troubles, God answered him out of the whirlwind. He accepted the submission of Job, who once or twice had been tempted to despair, and to forget the goodness of God, in the depth of his misery and

"AND GOD ANSWERED JOB OUT OF THE WHIRLWIND."

the greatness of his misfortune. God restored him to health and to his friends, and gave him more riches and comforts than he had before possessed. Truly, God can do all things; he may try us, but he can reward those who bear their trials patiently. May we all learn to say, with our whole hearts, "Thy will be done."

Half Hours with the Bible.

THE LIFE OF JESUS CHRIST, OUR SAVIOUR.

CHAPTER I.

THE BIRTH OF JESUS CHRIST.

MERRY Christmas and a Happy New Year to one and all of my little readers?

These are pleasant words and good wishes, such as we hope to utter and to listen to for many a year, trusting that these good wishes may be realised. But why is it, my young readers, that Christmas is such a joyous season? Not because the branch of holly trembles in the huge plum pudding, and the mince pies make their daily appearance on the dinner table, around which are gathered the father, the mother, and all the merry group of children, who spend the greater part of the year at some distant school; not because the rooms are decked with holly, and red berries mingle with ivy leaves in the old churches; but because on Christmas morning, smiling faces and glad voices sing with one accord that Christ was born in Bethlehem. Yes, this is indeed a festal day—the anniversary of a birthday that all Christians love to celebrate, and rejoice in the fulfilment of Isaiah's prophecy, saying, "Unto us a child is born, unto us a son is given: and his name shall be called Wonderful, Counseller, The mighty God, the Everlasting Father, The Prince of Peace."

I once heard of a dear little girl who was assisting some friends to decorate a Christmas-tree; and being told the toys and ornaments were intended as presents for the different members of the family, she anxiously inquired, "What present they could make to the Lord upon his birthday?" Some of you may think this a vain question, but many of you would doubtless be glad to have something worthy to offer to the Saviour; and so you have. There is only one thing which you could freely offer to Christ, that would satisfy and please him, and that is your hearts.

If you really love him, and lift up your hearts to him, feeble as they are, Jesus will accept and sanctify the gift. Perhaps you can repeat the hymn—

> Jesus Christ, my Lord and Saviour,
> Once became a child like me;
> Oh! that in my whole behaviour,
> *He* my *pattern* still might be.

THE LIFE OF JESUS CHRIST, OUR SAVIOUR. 267

THE BIRTH OF JESUS AT BETHLEHEM.

I do not know any sweeter words than these. What can be more wonderful than to know that the holy and almighty Saviour should come down into the world, in the form of a helpless child, like us, to suffer pain and weakness, and to feel hunger and thirst, and sorrow like unto ourselves? And what can furnish a more appropriate prayer for every reader, than the desire to copy Jesus in his whole behaviour and conduct? and what can afford us greater happiness, than to feel that Jesus, our pattern and our Redeemer, is also our friend, ever ready to hear us, and to help us, to pity and to intercede for us?

The birth of this wonderful child had been foretold by the different prophets many years before Christ really came upon the earth. Some foretold where he would be born, and others what would be his mission, and his sufferings; and just before his birth an angel was sent to Mary, the mother of Jesus, to tell her by what name the child should be called. Jesus, you know, means "a Saviour," and Christ signifies "the Anointed, the Messiah, or He that should come." You may remember that I told you how the kings were anointed with oil, and Christ, or "the Anointed," signifies that Christ was also "King of Heaven." At the time appointed by God the child Jesus was born, as the angel had foretold, and the mother of Jesus being away from home on a long journey, she was obliged to sleep in a stable where the oxen were kept, because there was no other room at liberty; and there God gave Mary the promised infant, who had no other bed for her sweet baby than the manger in which she laid him; but even here, while unnoticed and unattended, God sent wise men from a distant land to worship him. These wise and good men had heard, in their distant country, of the promised Saviour, and one evening, when they were gazing up into the heavens, they saw a very bright and peculiar star. God put it into their minds that this star would lead them to Christ; so they immediately went in the direction in which it appeared. This star went before them until it brought them near to Jerusalem, where Herod the king was living, and as they knew by inspiration that Christ was a king, they went to the palace to inquire, saying, "Where is he that is born King of the Jews? for we have seen his star in the east, and have come to worship him." Herod was alarmed at the idea of having a rival, but he did not say so; he merely inquired of the priests where Christ should be born, and when they told him "In Bethlehem," he advised the wise men to go and seek for the child there; and desired them to bring him word when they had found him. So the wise men again followed the star until it brought them to the feet of Jesus, and they rejoiced with exceeding great joy, and fell down and worshipped the infant Saviour; and they presented to him gold and frankincense and myrrh. Ah, my children, we need not travel a long way to seek the Saviour. He is always near—he can hear our softest prayer. He is our Saviour and our friend, and although he now sits at the right hand of God, he will be always ready to hear the praises of the youngest child. These men returned to their homes happy at having found the Christ; but the wicked Herod, who did not love the Saviour, was frightened lest he should lose his crown, and his power, and his riches, so he determined to kill the Lord Jesus, if he could. He sent his soldiers to Bethlehem, and desired them to kill every little baby in the town, hoping that one of these would be the promised king.

Many a poor mother's heart was grieved at the death of her helpless baby, killed by the soldiers; yet Herod was not able to kill Christ, because God put it into the mind of Joseph in a dream to arise by night, and take the young child and his mother into another country, called Egypt; so when the other poor babes were put to death Christ was in safety, and all his cruelty was vain. A successor of this wicked man, also named Herod, afterwards put to death a good prophet, called John the Baptist. This young man, who had been born to his parents in their old age, a few months before the birth of Christ, had been sent by God to be a forerunner or preacher about Christ.

CHAPTER II.

CHRIST'S BAPTISM AND FIRST MIRACLES.

WHEN Jesus was eight days old, he was carried to Jerusalem, and circumcised according to the law of the Jews, who did not baptize their children as the Christians do; and while he was in the Temple a very old man, named Simeon, was led by the Spirit to behold the Lord's Christ; and he rejoiced, and took the dear baby into his arms, and said, "Lord, now lettest thou thy servant depart in peace, for mine eyes

THE LIFE OF JESUS CHRIST, OUR SAVIOUR. 271

JOHN THE BAPTIST IN THE WILDERNESS.

have seen thy salvation." He meant that he was ready to die in peace, having seen the Saviour. A good old prophetess, named Anna, came into the Temple to worship God, and she also knew by inspiration, that it was her Saviour, and she blessed and praised God.

272 HALF HOURS WITH THE BIBLE.

JESUS WITH THE DOCTORS IN THE TEMPLE.

Twelve years after this, Jesus came up with his parents again to Jerusalem to keep the feast of the passover; but when Joseph and Mary set off to return home, Jesus stayed behind. As there was a large company of their friends and neighbors, Mary supposed that Jesus was with some other children; but when they stopped to rest at night, he was nowhere to be found. Joseph and Mary immediately turned back to Jerusalem, and after three days, they found Jesus sitting in the Temple with the most learned men, hearing them and asking them questions; and when Mary told him what sorrow his absence had occasioned them, he said, "Why did you seek me, wist ye not that I must be about my Father's business?" But although they understood not his meaning, Jesus obeyed the voice of his mother, and returned with her at once. In all things Jesus obeyed his mother's voice, and therefore he cannot love "a disobedient child."

I must now tell you a little more about John, who lived in the wilderness, and wore clothing made of camel's hair, fastened round his loins with a leathern girdle, living upon locusts, a kind of bean, and wild honey, he went about preaching, and saying, "Prepare ye the way of the Lord, and make his paths straight;" and he baptized all those who would listen to him, and believe in the coming of Christ. Even Jesus himself, because he wished to teach people to fulfil all the rites and mysteries of religion, went down to John to be baptized of him. John, knowing that Christ was without sin, answered that he had need to be baptized of Jesus, but when he found that Christ desired it he baptized him; and just as Jesus went up out of the water, the heavens were opened, and the Spirit of God descended like a dove upon him, and a voice was heard from heaven, saying, "This is my beloved Son, in whom 1 am well pleased."

Jesus soon after this went into one of the Jewish synagogues (or churches), and there he opened the book of the prophet Isaiah, and read where it was written, "The Spirit of the Lord is upon me, because he hath anointed me to preach the gospel to the poor; he hath sent me to heal the broken-hearted, to preach deliverance to the captive, and recovering of sight to the blind, to set at liberty them that are bruised, to preach the acceptable year of the Lord." So we must pray to Jesus to keep sin out of our hearts, and to pour his love into them instead. If we be holy, we shall be happy; and we can never pray too often, "Lead us not into temptation."

Jesus sat down upon the side of a high mountain, and began to preach to the people, saying:—

"Blessed are the poor in spirit: for theirs is the kingdom of heaven. Blessed are they that mourn: for they shall be comforted. Blessed are the meek: for they shall inherit the earth. Blessed are they which do hunger and thirst after righteousness: for they shall be filled. Blessed are the merciful: for they shall obtain mercy. Blessed are the pure in heart: for they shall see God. Blessed are the peace-makers: for they shall be called the children of God." And Jesus taught the people the little prayer which we say every day to "Our Father in heaven," and which is, on that account, called "The Lord's Prayer." About this time Jesus was invited to be present at a wedding feast, and there he is supposed to have wrought his first miracle. The bridegroom was probably a poor man, and unable to

CHRIST CHANGING WATER INTO WINE.

buy wine to set before his guests, and Mary, the mother of Jesus, said unto her son, "They have no wine." Jesus then privately desired the servants to fill the six stone waterpots with water, and when they had filled them, he desired them to draw out wine. The governor of the feast, having tasted the wine, was astonished, and he said unto the bridegroom,

"Every man at the beginning doth set forth good wine; and when men have well drunk, then that which is worse but thou hast kept the good wine until now." One day, a leper came and worshipped before him, saying, "Lord, if thou wilt, thou canst make me clean?" Jesus put forth his hand and touched him, and said, "I will; be thou clean," and the man was healed immediately; but Jesus sent him to show himself to the priests, and to offer the offering according to the law of Moses.

When Jesus was entering into Capernaum, a centurion (that is, a captain over one hundred soldiers) met him, and begged Jesus would heal his servant, who was sick of a disease called the palsy. Jesus said, "I will come and heal him." But the centurion answered, "Lord, I am not worthy that thou shouldest come under my roof; but speak the word only, and my servant shall be healed." Jesus himself was astonished at the faith of this good man, and he said to his followers, "I have not found so great faith, no, not in Israel." And he told the centurion to go his way, and as he had believed, so should his prayer be granted. The centurion went home quite happy, for he knew that Jesus could cure the sickness and sorrow of all who cry to him, and he found his servant quite restored to health.

CHAPTER III.

CHRIST IN THE TEMPLE, AND IN SAMARIA.

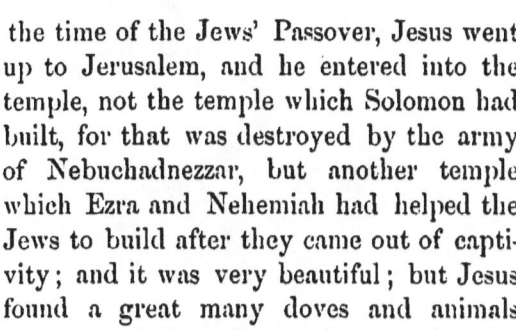

AT the time of the Jews' Passover, Jesus went up to Jerusalem, and he entered into the temple, not the temple which Solomon had built, for that was destroyed by the army of Nebuchadnezzar, but another temple which Ezra and Nehemiah had helped the Jews to build after they came out of captivity; and it was very beautiful; but Jesus found a great many doves and animals brought there and exposed for sale, so that people who wished to offer their sacrifices need have no trouble in procuring them, because they could buy them within the gates of the temple; and when Jesus saw this, he was displeased, and he cast out the buyers and sellers, and overthrew the tables of the money-changers, and the seats of those who sold doves; and he said unto them, "Take these things hence; make not my father's house an house of merchandise." He would not suffer the temple of his Father to be dishonoured, and he is displeased with all those who go to the house of prayer with worldly thoughts and feelings. And these sayings and doings of Jesus were much talked of by those who had seen him and his miracles; and one of the rulers of the Jews, a Pharisee, named Nicodemus,

CHRIST DRIVING THE MONEY-CHANGERS FROM THE TEMPLE.

thought a great deal about these things; he was a good man, and he wished to know what was good, and to see Jesus, but he was afraid to go to him openly, for fear of his proud and conceited brethren; so he came privately to Jesus by night, and said unto him, "Rabbi, we know that thou art a teacher come from God; for no man can do these miracles which thou doest, except God be with him." Jesus then explained to him that he must have a changed heart, and become a good and holy man, before he could hope to be a child of God. And Nicodemus went away with stronger faith, and more love to Jesus; and he afterwards became a disciple.

I must now tell you of some other miracles performed by Christ, as he went about from place to place doing good. One day he went into the house of Peter, and found the mother of Peter's wife very ill with a fever. Jesus went and touched her hand, and immediately the fever left her, and she got up and waited upon them: and he also cured a great many other sick persons before he entered into a ship with his disciples, with the intention of crossing the sea. Jesus was tired with preaching and walking so far, and he lay down on a pillow to sleep; but soon there arose a violent storm, and the ship was tossed up and down upon the waves, until the disciples, forgetting that Jesus was with them, and that they must be safe in his keeping, became so terrified that they awoke Jesus, saying, "Lord, save us: we perish." And he saith unto them, "Why are fearful, O ye of little faith?" Then he arose and rebuked the winds and the sea, and there was a great calm. You see one word from Jesus could bring peace and comfort: he said, "Peace" and all was still. This marvellous change astonished even those who had seen his miracles, and they

CHRIST AND THE WOMAN OF SAMARIA.

could not forbear saying, "What manner of man is this that even the winds and the sea obey him?"

On his way to Nazareth, Jesus had passed through Samaria; the weather was very warm, and Jesus sat down beside the well of Sychar, while his disciples were gone into the city to buy food. Jesus was hungry, weary, and thirsty, and as he sat there a woman came out of the city to draw water at the well. And Jesus said unto her, "Give me to drink." The woman was surprised that a Jew should ask water of a Samaritan woman, because the Jews despised the people of Samaria, on account of their having built a temple for themselves, after the Jewish captivity, when they had endeavoured to prevent the Jews from re-building one at Jerusalem. Jesus, however, was kind and good to the greatest sinners, and he said to the woman, "If thou knewest who it is that saith, Give me to drink, thou wouldest have asked of him, and he would have given thee living water, of which whosoever drinketh thirsteth no more." The woman said, "Sir, give me this water, that I thirst not, neither come hither to draw." The good Jesus then told her that he was the Messias, and that she must worship God in spirit and in truth.

CHAPTER IV.

CHRIST'S WONDERFUL DEEDS AND MIRACLES.

HEN Jesus came again to Cana, a rich nobleman came to him from Capernaum in great sorrow, because his dear son was so ill that the physicians said he must soon die, for they had tried in vain to make him better; and the weeping father, having heard of Jesus, came and begged the Saviour most earnestly that he would go to Capernaum and heal his son. Jesus did

THE NOBLEMAN AT CAPERNAUM.

not go: he wished to try the faith of the nobleman, saying, "Unless ye see signs and wonders, ye will not believe." The father was anxious that no time should be lost, so he again besought Jesus, saying, "Sir, come down, ere my child die." Jesus said, "Go thy way; thy son liveth."

THE MIRACULOUS DRAUGHT OF FISHES.

The nobleman believed the word that Jesus had spoken, and before he reached home he met his servant, who was coming to tell him the good news; and he inquired of his servant at what hour the child began to amend, and the servant told him that the fever had left the child at the seventh hour, which was the precise time at which Jesus had told the father that his son lived.

One day Jesus sat in a little ship belonging to one of

the disciples, and taught a large crowd of people who had followed him. Afterwards he told Simon to let down his nets into the sea for a draught; but Simon answered, "Master, we have toiled all night and taken nothing; nevertheless, at thy word I will let down the net;" and on doing so they caught such a multitude of fishes that their net brake; and Simon Peter was so much astonished that he threw himself at the feet of the Saviour, saying, "Depart from me, for I am a sinful man, O Lord." After this Jesus healed other sick, and some afflicted with evil spirits, and at Jerusalem he saw a sick man lying beside the pool of Bethesda. God used to send an angel to disturb the waters at certain times, and the first person who afterwards got into the pool was healed of his disease. This poor man had laid there thirty-eight years in pain and suffering, close to the pool, but, being too ill and weak to get into the water, some other sufferer, who had friends to assist him, would get in first, and the virtue of the water was gone. Jesus knew all this; he therefore came and asked the man, saying, "Wilt thou be made whole?" and the poor man no sooner expressed his wish to be cured than Jesus, who knew his heart, said, "Rise, take up thy bed and walk;" and, as the man went off with his bed, the loving Saviour warned him to leave off sinning, lest God should inflict a worse punishment upon him. Jesus had called together twelve men, who were called his apostles, and he used to teach these disciples many things in parables. A parable

CHRIST HEALING A SICK MAN.

is a kind of easy story which has two meanings; and the parables which were spoken by Christ, could only be understood by those to whom God gave the spirit of understanding. I will tell you some of these parables:—One was of the sower, who went out to sow his seed. Some fell by the wayside; some upon a rock, and was dried up; some among the thorns, that choked it; and some fell upon good ground, and flourished; and to his disciples he explained that the seed on the wayside were those who listened to

THE SOWER SOWING THE SEED.

the Gospel, and then went away and forgot what they had been taught; the seed on the rock are those who are penitent for a little while, but fall away at the first temptation to evil; the seed among thorns represented those who were too busy with their gains or their pleasures to attend; while the good seed where those who heard the word and kept it.

CHAPTER V.

CHRIST IS TRANSFIGURED, AND WALKETH ON THE SEA.

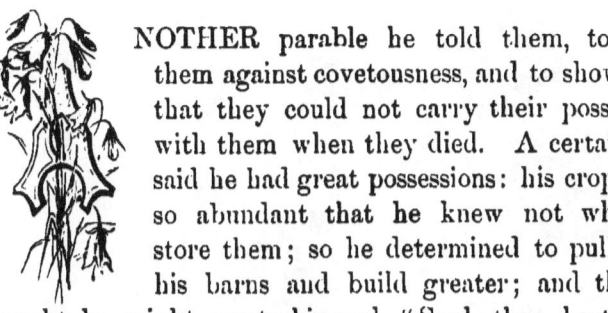

ANOTHER parable he told them, to warn them against covetousness, and to show them that they could not carry their possessions with them when they died. A certain man said he had great possessions: his crops were so abundant that he knew not where to store them; so he determined to pull down his barns and build greater; and then he thought he might say to his soul, "Soul, thou hast much goods laid up for many years; take thine ease, eat, drink, and be merry." But God said, "Thou fool, this night thy soul shall be required of thee: then whose shall those things be which thou hast provided?" So is he that provideth and careth for this world only. Another parable he told them of the man whose enemy sowed tares in the field with his wheat, and that at the harvest, or end of the world, the good people should be gathered like the wheat into the barn, or heaven, and the wicked, like the tares, should be burned in the fire. Jesus, having heard that John the Baptist had been put to death by Herod, went away in a ship to a desert place, followed by the poor whom he taught and comforted. When night came on, the disciples begged their Master to send the tired, hungry people back to their dwellings; but Jesus, knowing their wants,

288 HALF HOURS WITH THE BIBLE.

THE ENEMY SOWING TARES.

said, "Give ye them to eat." The disciples had only five loaves for themselves, and two small fishes. Yet Jesus commanded the multitude to sit down on the grass, and he blessed the food, and brake, and gave to the disciples, who gave to the multitude; and they all did eat, and were filled. And when all had eaten—about five thousand men, besides women and children—they gathered up twelve baskets full of pieces.

Jesus one day took three of his disciples with him on

THE MIRACLE OF THE LOAVES AND FISHES.

to a high mountain, and while there he became transfigured, or changed like a God, and his clothes looked white as snow, and his face was dazzling as the sun; and there appeared Moses and Elias, who talked with Jesus. Peter said, "Lord, it is good for us to be here;" and while he was speaking, a bright cloud covered them, and they heard a voice, saying, "This is my beloved Son, in whom I am well pleased; hear ye him." The disciples fell upon their faces with fear; but Jesus said, "Arise, and be not afaid;" and they lifted up their eyes, and found Jesus alone.

CHRIST IS TRANSFIGURED.

He soon after this performed a cure on the lunatic son of an unhappy father who had brought his child to Jesus for help and mercy. And when they came to Jesus to demand his share of the taxes paid to the Roman emperor, he was without money; but he sent his disciple Peter, and desired

CHRIST WALKING ON THE SEA.

him to cast a hook into the sea, and in the mouth of the first fish which came up he should find a piece of money sufficient to pay the demand made upon both. And scarcely was this done before they were followed by two blind men, who followed Jesus, crying, "Have mercy on us, O Lord, thou son of David." Nor were their cries in vain, for Christ restored to both their eye-sight.

It was on a dark and stormy night the disciples were trying to cross the sea in their little ship, but the wind and waves were both contrary. They were tossed about, and unable to get forward, when all at once they saw Jesus walking on the sea; but they knew him not, and were frightened, saying, "It is a spirit." But Jesus spake, saying, "It is I, be not afraid." Then Peter cried, "Lord, if it be thou, bid me come unto thee on the water." Jesus said, "Come." But as soon as Peter began to walk upon the water his faith failed him, and he began to sink, and he could only cry out, "Lord save me." And Jesus caught him by the hand, and said, "O thou of little faith, wherefore didst thou doubt?" And as soon as Jesus had come into the ship the storm ceased, and they were close to the land. He also spake the parable of the lost sheep and the prodigal son, the householder and his vineyard, and assured them that it was difficult for a rich man to enter into the kingdom of heaven. On one occasion he took a little child (for Jesus loved children, and was kind to them, and blessed them), and told his disciples that unless they became humble and guileless as a little child, they could not enter into the kingdom of heaven.

CHAPTER VI.

JESUS RAISETH THE DEAD.

HERE were two other miracles which Jesus performed that you will be surprised to hear of. He raised to life those who were dead, and one of these was a young girl; but the first was the son of a poor widow, who was following her only child to the grave, and weeping bitterly as she went. But Jesus met her at the gate of the city, and when he beheld her bitter grief, he said to her kindly, "Weep not." Then he touched the bier upon which the body was carried, and the bearers stood still, and Jesus said, "Young man, I say unto thee, Arise!" and he that was dead sat up, and began to speak, to the great joy of his broken-hearted mother. How happy was she to take him home again, and how much they ought to have loved the gentle and compassionate Saviour, who, not long after, restored to a sorrowing father his only child. Jairus was a ruler among the Jews, and a rich man, but his riches and power could not save his only child from death. When she was so ill that the doctors could do no more for her, her father ran to seek Jesus, but before he could bring him to his house a messenger was sent after him, saying, "Trouble not the master, for thy

294 HALF HOURS WIITH THE BIBLE.

THE RAISING OF JAIRUS'S DAUGHTER

child is dead." But Jesus bade him not to be afraid, only to believe. When they were come to the house, and heard the mourning and weeping, Jesus said, "Why make ye this ado and weep? the maiden is not dead, but sleepeth." And he went in, and took her by the hand, and said, "Damsel, I say unto thee, Arise!" And she arose, and walked, and did eat and drink, and was cured.

LAZARUS LYING SICK.

There was a family at Bethany whom Jesus loved—two sisters and a brother. One sister loved to hear of the things of God, when Jesus visited them; but Martha was always more anxious to wait upon Jesus. Lazarus their brother died, and although the sisters sent to Jesus, he did not go to them until Lazarus had been laid in the tomb four days. As soon as Martha heard that Jesus was coming, she ran out to meet him, and said, "Lord, if thou hadst been here, my brother had not died." But Jesus wept with them, and went with them to the grave; and the people were astonished to see Jesus weeping for Lazarus at the mouth of the cave; and he ordered them to remove the stone from the mouth of the tomb, and, after praying to his heavenly Father, he cried with a loud voice, "Lazarus, come forth!" And he that was dead came forth, tied up in his grave-clothes, and Jesus said, "Loose him, and let him go." How happy were the sisters to see their dear brother again, and how they must have loved and praised the gracious Saviour, who was soon going to lay down his life for them, and all other poor sinners, even little children! I have told you Jesus loved children, and when their mothers brought their little ones to him, Christ took them in his arms and said, "Suffer the little children to come unto me.'" And the kindest wishes that we can frame for the welfare of our young readers are, that they may learn to know and fear him, go to him with joy and gladness, and seek his blessing; for though he is now in heaven, he can bless them and keep them; and whoever inherits Christ's blessing here on earth, will be blessed for ever with the Saviour in heaven.

Half Hours with the Bible.

OUR SAVIOUR'S TEACHINGS AND SUFFERINGS

CHAPTER I.

HOW JESUS TAUGHT THE PEOPLE.

IT is, and must be, a great comfort to every one who can read the Bible, or who can hear it read, to know that the Bible is all true, and that it was given to us by a holy and just God, who cannot lie; and the faithful saying that God has given to us in it concerning his Son Jesus Christ is the most precious word that can be spoken.

We have heard many wondrous things the Lord has done for his people, since the creation of the world, and we have heard how many years the prophets and holy men of old prophesied, or foretold, the coming of Christ, and that he was to be the ransom for lost sinners: and we know that through the disobedience of our first parents all are born in sin, "the children of wrath;" and that only by the sacrifice of Jesus, the Lamb of God,

JESUS IN THE TEMPLE.

by faith in his death, we are made the children of grace; and that to all those who believe in the Lord Jesus, and in his gospel, will God grant forgiveness, mercy, and life everlasting. You must have heard how Jesus was born into the world a helpless baby, feeling all the pains and temptations that other children feel; and that he grew up among the children of this world, setting them an example of dutiful obedience to their parents, of love to our heavenly Father, of love to others, of gentleness, patience, meekness, and industry. All the time of his stay upon earth Jesus was never idle; he was always going about doing good, feeding the hungry, curing the sick, teaching the ignorant, reproving the wicked, comforting the sad and sorrowful, and sometimes raising the dead to life.

It would be almost impossible to hear of these wonderful works that Jesus did, to read of the parables and gracious words that fell from his lips, without feeling that he was indeed *the Christ*, the *Saviour* that should come into the world; and we ought to thank him every day of our lives that we are living in times when all these truths are being taught and acknowledged.

There were many things which Jesus taught his disciples which the proud Scribes and Pharisees would not understand; and he used to tell them little instructive stories called Parables. One of these was about an unkind servant. Peter had asked him how often he must forgive a person who had offended him, and Jesus told him seventy times seven. He meant very, very often; and if Peter did not forgive those who offended him, he could not hope God would forgive his many sins. So Jesus told his disciples of a certain king, whose servant owed him a very large sum of money, which he would never be able to pay;—even if he had been sold as a slave, with his wife and children, still the money would not pay the debt; so he fell down before the king, and prayed him to have patience with him, and he would pay him all. But the king forgave him the whole

300   HALF HOURS WITH THE BIBLE.

PARABLE OF THE UNKIND SERVANT.

debt. Not long after one of his fellow-servants got into his debt, when the unkind servant refused to listen to the excuses and prayers of his fellow-servant, but seized him rudely by the throat, and said, " Pay me that thou owest." The poor man was unable to do this, and the unkind servant cast him into prison. When his lord heard this he was angry, saying, "Oh, thou wicked servant, I forgave thee all that debt, because thou desiredst me: shouldst not thou also have had compassion on thy fellow-servant, even as I

THE LORD OF THE VINEYARD HIRING LABORERS.

had pity on thee?" Then the king delivered him to the tormentors, till he should pay all that was due to him. By this lesson Jesus teaches all to be kind and forgiving. One of his parables was of a house-holder who went out early in the morning to hire laborers into his vineyard: and he agreed to give them a penny a day. After this he hired other laborers, and some hours after he hired others, and quite late in the day he found others standing idle, and said unto them, "Why stand ye here all the day idle? Go ye also into the vineyard; and whatsoever is right that ye shall receive." So when the even was come, and the laborers came to be paid for their work, they received every man a penny. Then those laborers who had been hired early in the day were dissatisfied, because they had no more pay than the others, and they murmured against the goodman of the house, saying, "These last have wrought but one hour, and thou hast made them equal to us, which have borne the burden and heat of the day." But he answered them thus: "Friend, didst not thou agree with me for a penny? Take that thine is, and go thy way. Is it not lawful for me to do what I will with mine own?" And thus he taught them that to whom God will he is able to give the gift or wages of life eternal.

CHAPTER II.

PARABLES OF THE RICH MAN AND OF THE GOOD SAMARITAN.

THE parable of the rich man and Lazarus was told to the disciples to prevent them from seeking to be rich and prosperous in this world, and, above all, to be kind and charitable to the poor and afflicted. There was a rich man, who lived in a fine house, and had rich clothing, and the daintiest fare; but he took little heed of a poor beggar, named Lazarus, who,

LAZARUS AT THE RICH MAN'S GATE.

having no home, used to lie at the gate of the rich man's house, hoping to be fed with the broken pieces which the servants did not care to eat, for he was too sick to work or help himself. The very dogs took pity upon this poor man: they came and licked his sores, and tried to comfort him; but in all his pain he was happier than the rich man, for he loved God, and he looked forward to a better home in heaven, and when the angels came to carry him there, he would be happy for ever. And soon after the rich man died; he could only enjoy his riches and his good things as long as God gave him breath; and he had a grand funeral, and his body was laid in a fine tomb, and his soul was sent into a place of torment, where he could only look up to heaven, and see Lazarus resting on Abraham's bosom. In vain the rich man cried to Abraham for a drop of water to cool his burning tongue: he had carried no water to Lazarus in his suffering; he had only cared for himself; and now Abraham tells him that Lazarus, having suffered evils in his life with patience and submission, is rewarded; but that he, who had only cared for the riches, pleasures, and honors of the world, must now suffer for the bad use he had made of them. Then Jesus told them of the good Samaritan. You must remember that the Jews did not like the Samaritans: they considered themselves much better and holier; but Jesus wished to show them that their doings did not always agree with their professions; so one day, when the Jews were troubling Jesus with questions, hoping to make him say something contrary to their law, a lawyer asked him, saying, "Master, what shall I do to inherit eternal life?" Jesus, having asked him what was written in the law, told him that according to that law he must serve God, and love his neighbor. "Who is my neighbor?" questioned the wily lawyer; and Jesus answered in a parable, of a certain Jew, who, traveling from Jerusalem to Jericho, fell among thieves, and was stripped, robbed, wounded, and left half dead. The first who came by was

THE GOOD SAMARITAN.

a priest. He and a Levite also, seeing him, passed by on the other side. But a Samaritan bound up his wounds, poured wine into his parched lips, and, when sufficiently recovered, placed him on his own beast, accompanied him to the inn, and gave him in charge of the host, giving money, and promising more on his return. Then Jesus asked the lawyer, "Which of the three was neighbor to the man who fell among thieves?" The lawyer answered, "He who showed mercy." Then said Jesus, "Go and do thou likewise."

CHAPTER III.

PROPHECIES OF JESUS, AND MORE PARABLES.

ALL these things had been foretold by a prophet before the birth of Jesus, who now went into the Temple, and drove out those who were buying and selling in his Father's house. Jesus did not remain long at Jerusalem, but returned to Bethany. On the way thither he cursed a fig-tree that bore no fruit; and when they passed by again they found the fig-tree quite withered away already. I hope you are not like trees that produce no good fruit. He knows whether you love him. He knew that when the poor widow threw her two mites into God's treasury, that that one farthing was all the money she had in the world, and he praised her faith and love to his disciples. Surely the blessing of Jesus was worth more than all the gold and silver in the world. And soon after this Jesus saw his disciples admire the beautiful stones of the temple, and he told them that there soon should not be one stone left upon another. Then he took some of his disciples into a quiet place on the Mount of Olives, and explained to them some of the dreadful things that would happen to the beautiful city, and what should come to pass when he would come again in his glory at the end of the world. You will feel very shocked and sorry when you are old enough to read of the distresses that befell the Jews at the destruction of their fine city. And then he taught them again by parables. First he likened the kingdom of heaven to ten virgins, who took lamps in their hands, and went out to meet the bridegroom. Five of them were wise, and five of them were foolish virgins, who forgot to provide any oil in their lamps. At midnight—for in Jewish lands it is usual for marriages to be made in the evening—a cry was made, "Behold the bridegroom cometh. Go ye out to meet him." The virgins arose, and began to trim their lamps; but the foolish virgins, having no oil of their own, begged of the wise virgins, saying, "Give us of your oil, for our lamps are gone out." The wise virgins, however, having none to spare, told them to purchase oil for themselves. But while the foolish virgins were gone to buy oil, the bridegroom passed, and those who were ready went in with him to the marriage-feast, and the door was closed. In vain they cried at the door, "Lord, lord, open to us." The answer was, "I know you not." It was too late. Jesus, you know, is the bridegroom, the hour of whose coming is not known to us; the oil is the grace and love of God, and if our hearts are not filled with these when the Lord comes to call us to judgment, it will be too late to pray and repent afterwards. Only those who are prepared to meet him can go with Jesus to heaven. Another parable he told them of the good master, who gave talents (the money then in use in that country) to his servants—to one ten, to another two

THE PARABLE OF THE FEAST.

talents, and to another one—and the master went away; but, upon his return, he called the servants to give an account. The servants who had received five talents and two talents had made good use of their lord's money, and doubled it; while the other had hid his money in the ground, and the king punished him accordingly. Jesus also likened the kingdom of heaven to a certain king, who made a marriage for his son, and invited many guests to the marriage feast; but the invited guests paid no heed to

THE WEDDING GARMENT.

his kind invitation. So he sent his servants out into the highways and lanes, to bring in as many as they found, to partake of the feast. These poor people were all provided at the entrance with garments fit for a marriage feast; but when the king came in to see the guests, he found there a man who had not chosen to array himself in the beautiful dress. Then the king desired his servants to bind him hand and foot, and to cast him into outer darkness.

CHAPTER IV.

THE ENTRY INTO JERUSALEM.

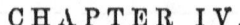ND now the time drew near when Jesus was to die, to be offered up as a sinless sacrifice for the sins of mankind, so he began his journey towards Jerusalem; and at Bethany, where Lazarus and his sisters dwelt, there was a feast made for Jesus by a rich man named Simon, and Mary sat down at the feet of Jesus. She had with her a box of very expensive ointment, with which she anointed his feet, and she wiped them with her long, soft hair. Judas, who was to betray the Saviour, grumbled at her, and thought it great waste to spend this valuable ointment in this way. He would have liked to sell it, and get the money, as he pretended, out of love to the poor. But Jesus, who could read all the thoughts of his heart, said, "Why trouble ye the woman? she hath wrought a good work upon me." And he went on to tell them that they could always find opportunities of doing good to the poor, for there were always poor people to be found who needed help and comfort; but that he was going to die, and Mary was anointing his body for burial, according to the custom of the country. And Jesus said, also, "Wheresoever this gospel shall be preached throughout the whole world, this also that she hath done shall be spoken for a memorial of her." But a

OUR SAVIOUR'S TEACHINGS AND SUFFERINGS.

great many of the people who were present were even then wishing for the death of Jesus; and some of them took counsel together to put Lazarus to death, because Jesus had raised him to life, and many people believed on the kind Saviour on that account. Jesus knew all their bad thoughts and desires, but he went on his way doing his Father's work. So the next day he sent his disciples forward from the Mount of Olives, and told them to go into the village, and they would find an ass tied and a colt by her, and that they should loose them and bring them to him; and as the disciples were untying the ass their owner inquired of them why they did so, and they said, "The Lord hath need of them;" and the man let them go. So they brought the ass to Jesus, and they spread their garments over it, and Jesus mounted thereon, to ride into Jerusalem. And when the people saw him coming they spread branches of trees, and possibly flowers, before him, and those who had fine garments spread them in the way, for the ass to walk over them, and they all cried and shouted for joy, saying, "Hosanna in the highest: Blessed is He that cometh in the name of the Lord!" There were many little children who joined in the cry, "Hosanna in the highest;" and Jesus was pleased to hear the little ones sing his praises. And when he came into the temple he found the people buying and selling doves, and a second time he drove them away from his Father's house, and desired them to keep it holy. A good prophet, named Zechariah, had foretold that Jesus

CHRIST'S ENTRY INTO JERUSALEM.

would come riding upon an ass lowly and humbly, although the king of heaven and earth. Jesus did not stay long in Jerusalem. He went to Bethany, and on the way he saw a fig-tree, which bore no fruit, and Jesus cursed the barren fig-tree, and immediately it withered away; and this will

OUR SAVIOUR'S TEACHINGS AND SUFFERINGS.

be the sad end of all who are not really good, but only pretend to do well that men may praise them. Jesus told his disciples some other parables. One was about a man who had a vineyard, and let it out to husbandmen, who refused to give their lord the fruit thereof, and they beat and ill-used his servants and his messengers. The owner then sent his own son, hoping that the husbandmen would honor and reverence him, but they did not, for they said, "Come, let us kill him." And they cast him out of the vineyard, and put him to death. When the lord of the vineyard heard this, he came and destroyed those wicked men, and let out their vineyard to others. In this parable Jesus reproved the wickedness of the Jews, who had killed the prophets, and foretold the salvation of the Gentiles, who should become Christians. We must try to obey God and love Jesus, if we would escape the punishment due to unbelievers. Another parable was of the prodigal son, who begged of his father to give him his portion, and he went away and spent it in rioting and extravagance. At last the money was all gone, his gay companions forsook him, and he was nearly starving with hunger. He was fain to eat the shells and husks that were given to the pigs, and he was very miserable when he thought of the happy home he had left. At length he determined to go back to his kind father, and tell him how sorry he was for his folly and wickedness. He said, "I will arise and go to my father, and will say unto him, Father, I have sinned against heaven

314　　　HALF HOURS WITH THE BIBLE.

THE PRODIGAL'S RETURN.

and before thee, and am no more worthy to be called thy son: make me as one of thy hired servants." Then Jesus points out the mercy of our Heavenly Father. He tells us that when the penitent sinner was yet a great way off the father saw him, and had pity on him, and went out to meet him, and kissed him, and even, while the sorrowing son confesses his guilt, the tender parent calls for a fine robe, and provides all his necessities, and makes a feast for very joy that his lost son is restored to him; and, when the elder brother murmured at the joyous welcome that was given to the wanderer, and turned away because he was too jealous to join in the merriment, his kind father came and begged him to go in, saying, "Thou art always with me, and all that I have is thine; but we must now make merry and rejoice over this thy brother, who was lost, and is found." How glad should we be when any poor sinner is brought back to the fold of God, for we know that the angels rejoice in heaven over penitent sinners!

CHAPTER V.

THE LORD'S SUPPER.

JESUS, with some of his disciples, went up into the Mount of Olives, near Jerusalem, and looked over the beautiful city; and there he foretold the sorrows that would come upon the Jews, and of wars, and famines, and troubles that would precede the destruction of the Jews; and there he promised his disciples to be with them in all their trials and sufferings for their Master's sake, and the destruction of Jerusalem would be a type of the coming of our Lord in power and glory. And not long after our Saviour's death the Romans came and besieged the city, inflicted unheard of cruelties upon the Jews, burned the holy temple, and totally destroyed the city, carrying away many captives. And Jesus told them of the day when he should come with his holy angels, and divide the sheep from the goats, putting the righteous on his right hand, and sinners on the left, and warned them to be ready at that day, the coming of which would be as a thief in the night. And all this time that Jesus was teaching his disciples, the wicked Judas was covenanting with the high priests to betray his master into their hands for thirty pieces of silver. It was just at the season when the Jews from all parts came up to Jerusalem to keep the feast of the passover, and to partake of the paschal lamb; and Jesus also came with his disciples, and he called two of them, and desired them to go into the city, where they would find a man bearing a pitcher of water, whom they should follow, and, entering into the same house, inquire of the good-man of the house, saying, "The master saith, where is the guest-chamber, where I shall eat the passover with my disciples?" and he would show them a room in which to prepare the feast. And the disciples went and found everything as Jesus had said, and when the passover was ready, Jesus came in the evening with his disciples to eat it. And while they were eating their supper Jesus was very sorrowful, for he knew all that was going to happen to him; and he said unto the twelve, "Verily, I say unto you, that one of you shall betray me." Most of the disciples wondered what their master meant, and questioned, saying, "Lord, is it I?" The Saviour answered that one

THE LAST SUPPER.

who dipped his hand in the same dish with him should betray him. Judas alone understood the Saviour's meaning, but he also pretended to wonder, saying, "Master, is it I?" Jesus answered, "Thou hast said." Then Jesus brake the bread, and blessed it, and gave it to the disciples, saying, "Take, eat, this is my body;" and he took the cup, and gave thanks, saying, "Drink ye all of it, for this is my blood, which is shed for the remission of sins." And since Jesus gave these his last commands to his disciples, all good Christians are happy to be allowed to partake of the Lord's

Supper. Then Jesus rose from the table, and took a basin of water, and washed the feet of his disciples, as an example to be lowly and humble. So they passed over the brook Cedron, and came into the garden of Gethsemane, and there Jesus left some of his disciples to pray, while he went on farther with three of his disciples, whom he desired to watch while he went on to pray by himself. While Jesus was praying, the tired disciples fell asleep; they could not see the large drops of sweat that fell in drops of blood from the Saviour's forehead. Three times he came back to his disciples, and found them sleeping, not watching and praying against temptation. Still he said kindly to them, "Sleep on now, and take your rest. Behold, he is at hand that doth betray me."

CHAPTER VI.

THE CRUCIFIXION.

SCARCELY had Jesus finished speaking when he saw Judas coming with a band of men, with swords and staves, to take him. Judas came up and kissed Jesus, saying, "Hail, master;" and immediately they laid hold of Jesus: he had not tried to escape. He said, boldly, "I am Jesus of Nazareth;" and they were so astonished at his majesty and gentleness, that some of them fell back-

OUR SAVIOUR'S TEACHINGS AND SUFFERINGS. 319

PETER SMITES OFF MALCHUS' EAR.

wards to the ground. One of the disciples drew a sword and smote Malchus, the servant of the high priest, and cut off his ear. The kind and gentle Saviour reproved Peter for his rashness, and although he knew the man to be his bitter enemy, he touched his ear and healed it; and the

PETER DENIES CHRIST.

disciples were so alarmed at the savage multitude that they all ran away and left Jesus, who was taken away to Caiaphas, the high priest. Peter, however, followed behind, trying to hide himself in the crowd. After he was come to the palace he was again taxed with being a Galilean, and Peter began to declare that he knew nothing of Jesus; but while he was speaking the cock crew, and Peter, remembering the words of his loving master, went out and wept bitterly for his ingratitude and his sin. Meantime some false witnesses, telling the priests that Jesus had spoken untruly, and the high priest asked Jesus what answer he could make. Jesus answered not a word until the high priest said, "Art thou the Christ, the Son of God?" Jesus answered, "I am; and hereafter you shall see me coming in the clouds of heaven;" but the high priest would not believe him. He cried out that Jesus was speaking blasphemy, and deserved to be put to death, and the people mocked and spat upon him; but Jesus, our example, bore these insults with meekness and patience: he was free from sin. But Judas, who had betrayed his Lord to death, when he knew that he was condemned, and saw him led away bound to Pontius Pilate, the Roman governor, felt very sad and miserable. The money gave him no peace: it reproached him so that he could not bear to look at or keep it. He brought the thirty pieces of silver back to the priests, and told them he had betrayed the innocent blood, but they felt no pity for him. They said, "See thou to that." So in his despair Judas threw down the pieces of silver in the temple, and went out and hanged himself. He did not weep and pray for pardon, as Peter had done; and his soul went to everlasting misery.

When Jesus was brought before the Roman governor, Pilate could find no fault in him, and wished to set him free; but he was afraid of offending the rich Jews, so he sent him to Herod, who questioned him, mocked and railed at Jesus, and sent him back to Pilate. The wife of Pilate had begged her husband not to condemn Jesus; but, although he knew him to be guiltless, he only tried to save himself from the blame, and he took water and washed his hands, saying, "I am innocent of the blood of this just man; see you to it." So the people cried out, "His blood be on us, and on our children." So Pilate, who feared man more than he feared God, gave the innocent Jesus into the hands of his enemies, and set free from prison a wicked thief named Barabbas. God did not free Pilate from blame, for we hear and read every day that Jesus was crucified, and suffered under Pontius Pilate. And the Jews have suffered many sorrows for their sins.

The soldiers then took Jesus, tore off his raiment, and put on him a purple robe; and they platted a crown of thorns, and put it upon his head, and made him hold a reed in his right hand for a sceptre; and they mocked him, bowing down before him, saying, "Hail, King of the Jews!" Then these cruel men smote him, and spat upon him, and insulted him, after which they put on his own raiment again, and led him away out of the city to crucify him. They made Jesus carry the large wooden cross upon his back; but when he was unable to carry the load any longer, they compelled a man named Simon, whom they met on the road, to carry it for him. The women, and many people to whom the Saviour had shown kindness, followed him in tears; and Jesus turned, and told them "Not to weep for him, but to weep for their own sorrows, and those

JESUS NAILED TO THE CROSS.

of their children." He knew what trouble was coming on them.

At last they came to Mount Calvary, and, on a spot called Golgotha, they drove large nails through his hands and his feet, and then they set the cross in the ground, and let Jesus hang upon it until he died.

While Jesus hung upon the cross he complained of thirst, but instead of giving him the spiced wine usual on such occasions, they gave him wine mingled with gall, and when Jesus had tasted the bitter cup, he would not drink. He was willing to bear all the pain for us, from nine o'clock in the morning until three in the afternoon. The soldiers took the garments and divided them among them, except the vesture, which was woven without a seam, and for this they cast lots, fulfilling the prophecy of David, saying, "They look and stare upon me; they part my garments among them, and cast lots upon my vesture." They then sat down and watched him, while many wicked men jeered him, saying, " He saved others, himself he cannot save;" while the gentle Saviour only pitied them, and cried, " Father, forgive them, for they know not what they do." Pilate wrote a title in three languages, and placed over the head of Jesus, "This is Jesus, the King of the Jews."

Again did he cry out, "I thirst;" and one of the soldiers gave him a sponge sopped in vinegar, on the top of a reed, to suck. When Jesus had received the vinegar, he said, "It is finished;" after which he cried, with a loud

OUR SAVIOUR'S TEACHINGS AND SUFFERINGS.

voice, "Father, into thy hands I commend my spirit," and he bowed his head and died.

There was a rich man called Joseph of Arimathea, who went to Pilate and begged the body of Jesus, so Pilate gave him leave to bury the body in his own tomb. So Joseph and Nicodemus took the body of Jesus down from the cross, and wrapped it in linen, with sweet scents and spices, and laid it in a new tomb hewn out in a garden, followed by the holy women, who had loved and honored the Son of God.

CHAPTER VII.

THE RESURRECTION OF JESUS.

ON the third day, as soon as the morning dawned, after keeping holy the Sabbath day, these good women came with spices to anoint the body of Jesus; but while they were considering how they should roll away the large stone that had been sealed over the door of the tomb, they saw that the stone was gone. Yes! The angel of the Lord had rolled away the stone, and the grave had given up its dead. Jesus was alive again, and an angel sat upon the stone, whose face shone like lightning, and his raiment was white as snow. Mary Magdalen left the other two

326   HALF HOURS WITH THE BIBLE.

THE RESURRECTION.

women while she ran back to tell the disciples that their Lord was risen, and the angel told the other women to go likewise and tell Peter and his disciples that Jesus was gone to Galilee.

You see Peter's sin had been forgiven, because he repented; and when he heard from Mary Magdalen that Jesus was not in the tomb, both he and John ran to the sepulchre, and saw the linen clothes lying empty, and then they believed that Jesus had risen again, so they went away, but Mary remained near the tomb weeping. Two

OUR SAVIOUR'S TEACHINGS AND SUFFERINGS.

angels clothed in white were sitting in the sepulchre, and they said to Mary, "Why weepest thou?" She answered, "Because they have taken away my Lord, and I know not where they have laid him." And as she turned round some one asked her the same question, "Why weepest thou?" Mary did not know that it was Jesus when she saw him, but she said, "Sir, if thou hast borne him hence, tell me where thou hast laid him, and I will take him away." Jesus saith unto her, "Mary!" She who so loved her Saviour knew his voice at once, and in tones of joy she answered, "Master;" She would have embraced his feet, but Jesus forbade her, and desired her to go and tell his brethren, saying, "I ascend to my Father, and to your Father; to my God, and to your God." Jesus afterwards appeared to the other two women, who fell down and worshipped him. The same evening he appeared to all his disciples, who were assembled together to prayer, and said unto them, "Peace be unto you;" and, having showed them the scars in his hands and his side, he breathed on them, and said, "Receive ye the Holy Ghost." Thomas, one of his disciples who was not present, refused to credit the glad tidings; but Jesus afterwards appeared to them again, and convinced Thomas that he was the risen Lord.

He appeared to other disciples and followers until forty days after his resurrection, and then he led them out once more to the village of Bethany, and promised them the gift of the Holy Ghost. and, having desired them to preach

CHRIST APPEARING TO HIS DISCIPLES.

the gospel through the world, he was suddenly taken up out of their sight, and ascended up into heaven, where He has promised to prepare a place for all who love and believe in Him. May our sins be washed away by his blood, and may we be ready to reign with him hereafter in glory!

Half Hours with the Bible.

THE STORY OF THE APOSTLES.

CHAPTER I.

OF THE DISCIPLES—ESPECIALLY THOMAS.

YOU do not require me to remind you, my dear little readers, that you have a dear Friend who loves and watches over you at all times, whether rich or poor; He is always at hand to help you, and He loves you more dearly than the kindest father. This Friend is Jesus Christ, who came down from heaven, and took upon him the form of a poor little helpless baby; who grew up to be a man, and taught us how to live, and to obey our Father in heaven, that we may go to be with Him when we die. You often say that "Christ was crucified for us, and He rose again from the dead;" and you read that He appeared to His disciples and many others before He ascended into heaven. His disciples were twelve poor men, whom He had chosen to be His friends, and to go about with Him and hear His teachings, and see His wonderful works that He performed, that they might be able to bear witness of the truth of His saying, and to teach others after He had gone back to heaven. One of these disciples, however, named Thomas, could not believe that Jesus had appeared to the other disciples in his absence; he could not understand, although he had seen our Saviour restore others to life, that Jesus should be alive again. With two of his disciples, he had taken a long walk, explaining to them the meaning of many wonders, which they had not before understood; and when they arrived at a place called Emmaus, He had sat down with them to supper; but they knew not who it was that talked with them until Jesus took the bread, and brake it, and blessed it. Then their eyes were opened, and they knew their Lord again. But Thomas could not believe these things. He said, "Except I put my finger into the print of the nails, and thrust my hand into his side, I will not believe." Now Jesus loved Thomas in spite of his unbelief; so He came again when the disciples were all met together for prayer, and He stood in the midst, although the doors were close shut, and said, "Peace be unto you." Then he repeated the very words of Thomas, saying, "Reach hither thy finger, and behold my hands; and reach hither thy hand, and thrust it into my side; and be not faithless, but believing." And the humbled and believing Thomas an-

THE STORY OF THE APOSTLES. 331

THE UNBELIEF OF THOMAS.

swered, "My Lord and my God." *You*, my little children, cannot in this world see Jesus; but you may believe that He is also your Lord and your God; and you must love Him and believe in the Son of God, "that believing, ye might have life through His name." Thomas did this afterwards. He is said to have travelled through Persia and India, preaching about Christ; and there he was, many years after, put to death by the idolatrous priests. Jesus then appeared to some of his disciples, who had been all night fishing, without being able to catch anything. The disciples did not know their Lord until He bade them "cast their net on the right side of the ship," which instantly became filled with a hundred and fifty-three large fishes. He then fed them with some of the fishes, which they broiled over a fire, and with bread; and having dined, Jesus gave them good counsel, and prophesied unto them, until they were fully convinced that Jesus was indeed the very Christ who had been raised up on the cross for them. A few days after, when they were all assembled with Him, a short distance from Jerusalem, He ascended up into heaven, and a cloud received Him out of their sight. And they all returned to Jerusalem, where they appointed a new disciple in the place of Judas Iscariot, who had betrayed Christ, and afterwards hanged himself, in despair for what he had done. On the day of Pentecost, one of the feasts of the Jews, these disciples were all gathered together for prayer, when suddenly there came a wondrous sound, like a rushing mighty wind, that filled the house; and tongues of fire appeared to rest upon the head of each of them, and they were enabled, by the mighty power of God, to speak and preach in different tongues and languages, such as they had never heard or understood before.

All the Jews who saw and heard this wonderful miracle were astonished; but Peter stood up boldly, and preached to them of Jesus, until many of them repented, and were baptized by the disciples, and were received as members of the Church of Christ.

CHAPTER II.

OF PETER AND JOHN.—ANANIAS AND SAPPHIRA.

PETER and John went one day into the Temple to pray. At the entrance-gate, called "Beautiful," lay a poor lame man, who had only the charity of those who entered the gate to subsist upon. He had been carried there as usual, and began to ask alms of Peter and John. These disciples were themselves poor, but they had something better than money to bestow. So Peter said to the poor cripple, "Look on us;" and as he gazed earnestly on them, Peter said, "Silver and gold have I none; but such as I have give I thee." And taking him by the hand, he lifted him up, saying, "In the name of Jesus Christ, rise up and walk." And instantly strength was restored to his ancle bones; he stood, and walked, and entered the Temple of God, leaping, walking, and praising Him. And all who saw this miracle were astonished. But Peter explained to them that not by their own power or holiness had they given the lame man ability to walk, but that God had done this miracle by His own power and mercy; and he preached to them of Christ crucified, and touched their hearts; so that about five thousand more were added to the Church. The Sadducees, and the high priest and others, being griev-

PETER HEALING THE LAME MAN.

ed that the disciples taught the people, had Peter and John brought before them, and questioned them; but not being able to punish them, they commanded them not to teach in the name of Jesus. But Peter prayed to God so earnestly that God would give them boldness and grace to preach and perform miracles in His name, that the place they were in was shaken, and they were all filled with the Holy Ghost, and most of those present were convinced of the truth of their preaching; and they sold their houses and lands, and gave the money for the use of the disciples.

THE STORY OF THE APOSTLES.

And now comes a sad story. A man named Ananias, who wished to appear as good and noble as the rest, went and sold a piece of land; and keeping back a part of the money, he took the remainder, and laid it at the apostles' feet. Now God had given His disciples power to understand many hidden things, as well as to speak in foreign tongues; and Peter knew quite well what Ananias had done, so he said unto him, "Ananias, why hath Satan filled thine heart to lie to the Holy Ghost, and keep back part of the price of the land? Thou hast not lied unto men, but unto God." And as Peter said these words, Ananias fell down dead at his feet, and some young men carried out the body, and buried it.

His wife Sapphira knew quite well what had been done with the money, and she soon after came into the presence of the apostles, not knowing of her husband's death, and Peter asked her, saying:—"Tell me, did you sell the land for so much?" and she answered, "Yea, for so much."

But Peter said, "How is it that ye have agreed together to tempt the Spirit of the Lord? Behold the feet of them which have buried thy husband are at the door, and shall carry thee out." Then Sapphira also fell down, and died instantly, and they carried her out, and buried her beside the body of her husband; but their souls were gone: not up to heaven to be with Jesus, but to Satan, who is the father of lies, and who had tempted them to lie. All who saw these things were in great fear; and many believed.

CHAPTER III.

THE FIRST MARTYR.

THE word martyr signifies a person who dies in defence of his religion, and many of the first followers of the Lord were martyred, or put to death, for loving Jesus, and teaching in his name. The disciples had chosen, from among the many newly converted Christians, seven holy and wise men, who were called deacons, to assist them in visiting the sick, and giving alms to the needy; and one among them, named Stephen, did many miracles and wonders; for God had sent the Holy Spirit into his heart, and the poor loved Stephen. But the powerful enemies of Christ rose up against Stephen, and accused him of preaching things contrary to their law. When Stephen stood up to defend himself, he looked so calm and holy, that his face appeared like "the face of an angel." He told them all the things that had been foretold of Jesus by Moses and the prophets; and that destruction would come upon those who rejected and denied their Saviour, and put him to death. His enemies, the greatest of whom was a young man, named *Saul* (who afterwards became a Christian himself), grew so angry, that he bade the people cast great stones at him to kill him. Even in his sufferings, the good and gentle Stephen prayed for his murderers, following the example of our blessed Saviour. Stephen

THE MARTYRDOM OF STEPHEN.

prayed, looking up to heaven, "Lord Jesus, receive my spirit;" and kneeling down, he cried with a loud voice, "Lord, lay not this sin to their charge!"

Stephen died peacefully, very. His friends buried him with great mourning; but Saul and his enemies treated them so cruelly that they were all obliged to separate, and leave Jerusalem.

THE SIN OF SIMON THE SORCERER.

Philip went to Samaria. Many of the Samaritans were converted, and one of them, a sorcerer, also joined himself with the believers and was baptized. Simon wished to work miracles; he offered money to the disciples, that they might give him the Holy Ghost, and enable him to bestow it on others. Peter, however, reproved him sharply, saying, "Thy money perish with thee, Simon, because thou hast thought the gift of God can be bought with money."

In a distant country called Ethiopia, lived the officer of

THE STORY OF THE APOSTLES. 339

PHILIP AND THE EUNUCH.

a great queen, named Candace; and this eunuch, or officer, was returning from Jerusalem in his chariot, reading very attentively the prophecies of Isaiah. And God sent Philip to the side of the chariot, and he asked the officer if he understood the meaning of the words he was reading? The eunuch answered, "That he required some one to explain it to him," and Philip, getting into the chariot, taught the officer about Jesus; and the eunuch understood and believed; and when they came to some water Philip baptized him.

CHAPTER IV.

DORCAS.

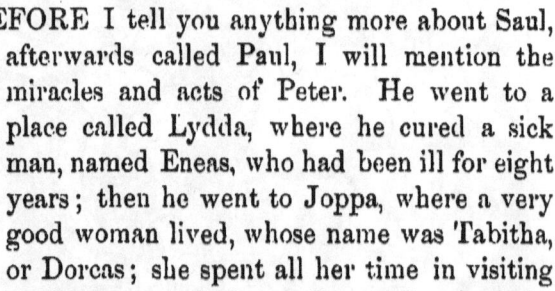

BEFORE I tell you anything more about Saul, afterwards called Paul, I will mention the miracles and acts of Peter. He went to a place called Lydda, where he cured a sick man, named Eneas, who had been ill for eight years; then he went to Joppa, where a very good woman lived, whose name was Tabitha, or Dorcas; she spent all her time in visiting and working for the poor and the needy, until at last she fell sick and died: and all the poor people in Joppa were grieved at her death.

When Peter heard this he went directly to the house, where the friends of Dorcas were weeping over her dead body. And the poor widows were showing each other the coats and garments Dorcas had made for them. So Peter sent them all away, and prayed to God that he would restore Dorcas to life again. He took her by the hand, and said, "Tabitha arise;" and God answered the prayer of Peter, for she opened her eyes and sat up, and Peter restored her to her friends, alive and well, because God loved Dorcas, for her charity and kindness to the poor.

Herod, the wicked king of Judea—having put to death with the sword James, the brother of John—heard soon

THE STORY OF THE APOSTLES.   341

THE RAISING OF DORCAS.

after that Peter was come to Jerusalem; so he caught him and put him in prison, with a number of soldiers to guard him safely. But God heard the prayers of his people, and did not suffer Peter to be killed just then. The night before he was to be tried, Peter lay sleeping in the prison, bound with two strong chains, and soldiers guarding the door, suddenly a light shone in the prison, and an angel bade him "Arise up quickly. Gird thyself (which meant dress thyself), and follow me." Peter's chains fell off, and he rose up, and put on his garments, and followed the angel,

PETER DELIVERED FROM PRISON.

believing that it was a vision. They passed through the doors until they came to the iron gate that led into the city; and the gate opened of its own accord, and Peter and the angel passed through, and down one street, and then the angel disappeared. Peter soon came to himself, and said, "Now I know of a surety that the Lord hath sent his angel, and hath delivered me out of the hand of Herod;" and after a little thought he walked straight to the house of Mary, the mother of Mark, at whose house were assembled several Christians, who were mourning and praying for Peter. First they feared that Herod had put him to death, and that his spirit had appeared to them; but, when the knocking continued, they joyfully admitted Peter, and listened to all that God had done to deliver him. Peter then bade them "Go and tell the good news to the brethren;" and he departed to another place. Herod and the Jews were very wroth when they found Peter had escaped; and Herod cruelly put the keepers of the prison to death; but God punished Herod for his wickedness. One day he sat on the throne, dressed in his robes, and made a fine speech; but God struck him with a fearful illness, and he soon after died a very miserable death: and Peter, after preaching many years, was crucified, as Jesus had foretold.

CHAPTER V.

THE STORY OF PAUL.

THERE was a rich and clever young Jew of Tarsus, who studied the law at Jerusalem, under Gamaliel, and he became very learned, and was very strict in keeping the laws of Moses, and thought himself very righteous. So when he first heard of Jesus and his followers, he despised and rejected Him, and persecuted every one who loved and believed

THE CONVERSION OF SAUL.

in the Saviour. He went to Damascus, to hunt out the Christians there, and put them to death. But God in his mercy had other work for Saul; so God met him on his journey. On a sudden a great light shone from heaven, and Saul fell to the ground. He heard a voice crying, "Saul, Saul, why persecutest thou me?" And Saul said, "*Who art thou?*" And the Lord said, "I am Jesus, whom thou persecutest."

Saul, trembling and astonished, asked, "Lord, what

wilt thou have me to do?" And the Lord said unto him, "Arise and go into the city, and it shall be told thee what thou must do." Blinded, dazzled, and astonished, Saul arose from the earth, and was obliged to be led by those who journeyed with him, and who were also dismayed at hearing the voice when no person was visible; and they brought Saul to Damascus, where he continued three days, without sight and without food. Then a certain good man, named Ananias, to whom the Lord appeared in a vision, and gave him instructions what to do, came in search of Saul. Ananias entered into the house, and, putting his hands upon him, said, "Brother Saul, the Lord, even Jesus, that appeared to thee in the way as thou camest, hath sent me that thou mightest receive thy sight, and be filled with the Holy Ghost." And Saul received his sight instantly, and arose and was baptized, and partook of some food, and continued some days with the disciples at Damascus, where he boldly preached Christ in their synagogues, to the astonishment of all those who heard the late persecutor of Christ's followers telling that Jesus was indeed the Son of God. Saul was persecuted in his turn by the Jews; and the disciples, in order to save his life, were obliged to drop him over the wall of the city in a basket. So Saul escaped to Jerusalem; but the disciples were at first afraid to receive him, until Barnabas took him by the hand, and immediately Saul disputed with the Grecians, and boldly and openly taught that Jesus was the Saviour of the world.

CHAPTER VI.

ELYMAS THE SORCERER.

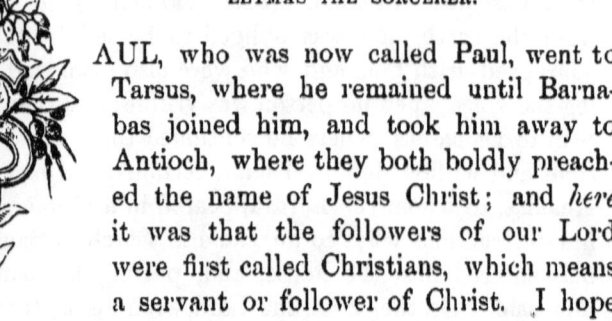

SAUL, who was now called Paul, went to Tarsus, where he remained until Barnabas joined him, and took him away to Antioch, where they both boldly preached the name of Jesus Christ; and *here* it was that the followers of our Lord were first called Christians, which means a servant or follower of Christ. I hope none of my little readers are ashamed of this name, but that they really and truly mean to be Christians, as Paul was. The disciples at Antioch sent money, by the hands of Paul and Barnabas, to the poor Christians at Jerusalem, who, when they finished their work, returned again to Antioch, and from thence the Holy Spirit sent them to preach at other places. At Paphos, in the Isle of Cyprus, they found a governor, named Sergius Paulus, who wished to be good and wise, and he listened to the preaching of the disciples; but there was also a very wicked man, called Elymas, who hated the truth, and wished to prevent others from hearing it. Then Paul, looking earnestly on him, said to Elymas, "Thou child of the devil, behold the hand of the Lord is upon thee, and thou shalt be blind, not seeing the sun for a season." And his sight was gone immediately, so that he was obliged to be led by the hand; and all

THE STORY OF THE APOSTLES. 347

THE SACRIFICE AT LYSTRA.

who saw this miracle were astonished, and many believed on the Lord Jesus; but in some places they were driven out, fearing they might be stoned to death. At Lystra, Paul had mercy upon a poor cripple and healed him, which, when the people beheld the lame man walking and leaping, they brought oxen decked with garlands to sacrifice unto the disciples, believing that they were gods. Paul and Barnabas, however, rent their clothes, and ran among the people, crying, "Sirs, we are but men of like passions with yourselves, who seek to turn you from the vanities of earth to serve the living God," but with great difficulty they kept the people from offering sacrifices unto them. Meanwhile, some of the Jews, their enemies, came from Antioch, and persuaded the people that they were wicked men, and they stoned Paul, and then dragged him out of the city, supposing that he was dead. But as the disciples stood mourning around him, God gave Paul strength, and he arose and went back into the city.

The vision of a man from Macedonia seemed to cry unto Paul, saying, "Come over into Macedonia, and help us." So Paul answered this appeal by starting at once to Philippi, where he began to teach and to preach, and he accosted the women who resorted to the side of the river, where they sometimes met for prayer. And God touched the heart of Lydia, a seller of the fine purple linen of those days, and made her attend to the words of Paul; so she became a Christian and was baptized, and all her household; and she invited the disciples to lodge at her house, which they did for a season, but again the Lord suffered them to be persecuted for His name's sake.

So the multitude rose up against the disciples, and the magistrates rent off their clothes, and commanded that they should be beaten. And having beaten them very cruelly, they cast them into the prison, desiring the jailor to keep them safely. This man was cruel and hard-hearted, so he put them into the inner prison, and made their feet fast in the stocks, so they could not move. But although they were chained and unable to help themselves, they were still able to call upon God, for whose sake they had borne all this suffering. They were in too much pain to sleep; they could not lie down; but they could still pray to God and praise him; so they sang praises to God at midnight, and their hymns of praises were heard by the other prisoners, when all on a sudden the whole prison was shaken by a great earthquake, so that all the doors which had been fast bolted flew open, and the chains fell off from the prisoners. The keeper of the prison, being startled out of his sleep, and seeing all the doors open, was in a great fright, fearing the prisoners had escaped; he knew that he would be very severely punished if such were the case, and he got a sword and was going to kill himself at once. But Paul, who, by the Spirit of God, knew all things, cried out to him in the dark, "Do thyself no harm, for we are all here." Then the jailor, knowing that this was the work of God, called for a light, and sprang in trembling, and fell down before Paul and Silas. Then he brought them out, and said, "Sirs what must I do to be saved?"

And they said, "Believe on the Lord Jesus Christ, and thou shalt be saved, and thy house." And they spake to him, and to all his household, the words and works of the Lord.

Then was the jailor sorry for his cruelty to his prisoners; so he took them the same hour of the night, and he bathed the wounds that had been made upon them when they were beaten; and behaved kindly to them; and he was baptized, he and all his family, and he brought the disciples into his own house, and set meat before them, and rejoiced in the Lord, in whom he believed. See how easy it is for the love of God to change the heart. A few hours before, this jailor hated Paul, and did everything to hurt and grieve him; but now he was gentle, and sorry for his unkindness, and anxious to do everything to please God. He had found out the only way to be saved is to believe in the Lord Jesus Christ. The earthquake had frightened others besides the jailor and the prisoners; the magistrates were frightened; they wanted to get rid of these strangers, so in the morning they sent to the jailor desiring him to let them go. Then the keeper of the prison came at once to Paul, saying, "The magistrates have sent to let you go; now therefore depart, and go in peace." But Paul said unto them, "They have beaten us openly, uncondemned, being Romans, and have cast us into prison; and now do they thrust us out privily? nay, verily, but let them come themselves and fetch us out." The magistrates were in great fear when they heard that they were Romans whom they had beaten so unceremoniously, so they came to the prison, and besought them and brought them out, and begged them also to leave the city, which, after visiting the house of Lydia, and comforting the brethren, they did, passing through Amphipolis and Apollonia to Thessalonica; and

THE STORY OF THE APOSTLES. 351

PAUL PREACHING TO HIS FRIENDS.

there the preaching of Paul for three Sabbath-days added many to the Church. Paul was obliged to depart into Athens, where his heart was grieved at the idolatry of the people, and he commenced at once teaching and preaching the name of Jesus. So they brought Paul before the court of philosophers, or wise men, and asked him what these things meant, and Paul told them that the "unknown God" to whom they had built an altar was Lord of heaven and earth, and he told them that Jesus would come to judge them.

CHAPTER VII.

THE DEEDS OF ST. PAUL.

THERE was a Jew named Aquila, who, with his wife Priscilla, had been banished from Rome because they were Christians, and they had gone to live at Corinth, whither Paul journeyed, and on his arrival at their city they received Paul very kindly; and as they had all to work for their daily bread, Paul lived with them, and worked at tent-making. There was one season of the year when the Jews all left their houses and dwelt under a tent, and they call this the feast of tabernacles; and Paul made tents for the Jews on the week days, but on the Sabbath-days and at other seasons he preached in their synagogues, and instructed both Jews and Greeks. Crispus, the ruler of the synagogue, and many others, became followers of Christ; but Paul had also his enemies. God, however, comforted Paul by a vision, bidding him "not be afraid, but to speak boldly." And when they brought him before Gallio, the Roman governor, he could see that they had a spite against Paul, and Gallio would not listen to them or punish Paul. During his stay at Corinth, Paul wrote several letters or epistles to the different churches, and he afterwards wrote to the Corinthians, for he loved them very much. At Ephesus, Paul parted from his friends Priscilla and Aquila, and during his

THE STORY OF THE APOSTLES.

absence a young Jew, named Apollos, learned a great many good things from them; and he, being a true Christian, was very thankful for their instructions, and he soon became a very useful preacher, and went away, like St. Paul, to teach those who knew not Christ. After the return of Paul to Ephesus, some of the unbelieving Jews pretended to heal diseases and work miracles, like that apostle; and they pretended to cure one man who had an evil spirit, but the man cried out, "Who are ye? Jesus I know, and Paul I know, but who are ye?" He knew that they were not holy men and followers of Christ, so he rushed upon them, and wounded them, so that they were glad to escape with their lives. And this so much terrified those who had done the like, that they came to Paul and burnt all their wicked books, and no more pretended to work magic and sorcery. But in a short time so many of the people became Christians, that the silversmiths who made little images of Diana, whom they called their goddess, had no sale for their images, because the people worshipped Jesus instead of Diana. Wherefore one of these smiths, named Demetrius, made a great uproar in the city against Paul, and a great crowd of people ran about, crying, "Great is Diana of the Ephesians!" And they tried to get hold of Paul, until the town clerk came out and addressed the people, advising them to be quiet, and to let Demetrius carry the matter to the law. At length the people dispersed, and Paul took leave of his friends, and once more went forth on his mission. One evening, when a company of Christians were gathered together at Troas to hear Paul, there sat beside one of the high windows a young man, named Eutychus, listening to his discourse; but Paul (being anxious to say a great deal in the short time he was with them) preached till past midnight, and Eutychus, falling asleep, overbalanced himself, and fell down, being picked up for dead. This caused much sorrow and dismay among the disciples; but Paul said, "Trouble not yourselves, for his life is in him," and he embraced Eutychus, and brought him alive again, to the joy and comfort of all; and when he had given them the sacrament, Paul took leave of them, and went away at day-break to Miletus, where he appointed to meet some of the disciples on his way to Jerusalem. And after warning them and praying with them, he bade them farewell; but they all wept sore, and clung about him, and kissed Paul and Silas, and went with them even to the ship, for they were grieved at their departure.

At Cesarea Paul dwelt in the house of Philip the evangelist, who had four daughters who did prophesy. And a prophet named Agabus came thither, and binding his hands and feet with Paul's girdle, foretold what should happen to him at Jerusalem; wherefore his friends wept and tried to persuade Paul not to go there. But Paul would not be turned from his duty. He went, but he had no sooner began his mission than the unbelievers drew Paul out of the Temple and tried to kill him, and they beat and ill-treated

DEPARTURE OF PAUL FOR JERUSALEM.

him, as they had done our Saviour. At length the chief captain got him safely to the castle, and then, having permission to speak, Paul told them all his history. The Jews heard him for some time patiently; but when he began to tell of Jesus, they would not listen, and again began beating Paul, until they found he was a Roman; and then he was ordered to appear before the council, where he defended himself. Ananias, the hight priest, commanded them to smite him on the mouth. Paul cried out to Ananias, "God shall smite thee," for breaking the law, while pretending to judge according to the law.

CHAPTER VIII.

FESTUS AND PAUL.

FESTUS, the new governor, having heard about Paul from the Jews, commanded the prisoner to be brought before him. Paul again answered for himself that "he had done nothing contrary to the Jewish law, and that having been unjustly imprisoned for two years, he would now be judged by Cæsar, the Roman Emperor, being himself a Roman." Festus said, "Hast thou appealed unto Cæsar? unto Cæsar shalt thou go." But after some days King Agrippa, with his sister Bernice, came to Cesarea to see Festus, and Festus having told Agrippa a great deal about Paul, they became very anxious to see him; so the next day, when all the nobles and captains were assembled in the place of hearing, Paul was brought before them. Then Agrippa said unto Paul, "Thou art permitted to speak for thyself." Paul was always glad to have the chance of telling what Jesus had done for him, so he told them his whole story; how, from being a persecutor, God had called him to bear witness of the Lord Jesus, of whom Moses prophesied, who had suffered and risen again from the dead. When he heard this, Festus cried out, "Paul, thou art beside thyself: much learning doth make thee mad." But Paul answered calmly that his words were "words of soberness and truth;" and

THE STORY OF THE APOSTLES.   357

PAUL BEFORE AGRIPPA.

he turned to the king and said, "King Agrippa, thou knowest these things. Believest thou the prophets? I know that thou believest." And Agrippa felt the power of Paul's words, for he answered, "*Almost* thou persuadest me to be a Christian!" And Paul said, "I would to God that all who hear me this day were as I am, except these bonds." So the king and all rose up, and decided that Paul had done nothing wrong; but that, as he had appealed to the Emperor, he must be sent to Rome. So Paul and some other prisoners were sent in a ship under the care of a centurion. When they had got part of the way, Paul, finding it very stormy, tried to persuade the captain to stay there for the winter; but no one would listen to Paul, and in a few days a great wind arose and wrecked the ship. But the Lord comforted Paul, and he stood up and bade his companions "fear not, for the angel stood by me this night, and hath given me the lives of all who sail with me; nevertheless we must be cast on a certain island." All that Paul said came true; the ship was driven on the rocks at Melita, and all broken to pieces; but some of them managed to swim ashore, others in boats or on planks and fragments of the ship; all got safely to land.

The island of Melita, now called Malta, was inhabited by heathens; but although ignorant, they were very kind to Paul and his shipwrecked companions, and they lighted a fire of sticks to warm them, for it was very cold, rainy weather. Paul gathered some sticks together and threw on the fire, and a viper, which had been concealed among them, sprang up, and fastened on his hand. The people knew that the bite of the viper was poisonous, and expected to see Paul fall down dead, but God did not permit him to be hurt; he shook the viper off into the fire, and felt no harm. The people thought he must be a god, when they saw this miracle; but Paul soon taught them about Jesus, and he cured the father of Publius, one of the chief men of the island, who was sick of a fever.

PAUL AT MELITA.

Three months after this Paul left Melita, and sailed in another ship to Rome, where he was kindly received, and allowed to live in a house by himself, where many Jews were converted. Here he wrote most of his epistles, and a few years after he was put to death for the love of his Saviour, with whom he now lives in heaven, where Christ is gone to prepare a place for those who believe in his name.

Most of the disciples suffered also in the service of their Divine Master. The apostle who lived longest was John.

the disciple whom Jesus loved, and to whose care he had given his mother, when dying on the cross. After being cruelly persecuted, he was banished to an island in the sea called Patmos, where he lived in a cave or grotto, which is still shown to visitors as the place where he wrote his Epistle to the Seven Churches, his three Epistles, and a wonderful book called the Revelation, because it is the history of things which were revealed to him by the Holy Spirit in a vision. One in the form of the Saviour appeared there to comfort him, and he told John what to write to the Seven Churches, which have now most of them passed away. John saw, in his vision, the Lord sitting on his throne with a rainbow round his head, and in the midst of the throne was a Lamb as it had been slain—the Lamb of God, that taketh away the sins of the world—and all round the throne were the redeemed and happy people, clothed in white and with golden crowns upon their heads. John afterwards left Patmos, and died at Ephesus, a very old man. In his epistles he begs all little children "to love one another," and as long as he lived he tried to teach others the way to heaven. And I trust all those who may read these "Half-hours with the Bible" may one day join that glorious throng, and sing with them that holy song, saying, "Amen. Blessing, and glory, and wisdom, and thanksgiving, and honour, and power, and might be unto our God for ever and ever. Amen."

www.ingramcontent.com/pod-product-compliance
Lightning Source LLC
Chambersburg PA
CBHW020241240426
43672CB00006B/596